G000272684

The Mercedes-Benz since 1945
Volume 3

The Mercedes-Benz since 1945

Volume 3: The 1970s

A collector's guide
by James Taylor

MOTOR RACING PUBLICATIONS LTD
Unit 6, The Pilton Estate, 46 Pitlake, Croydon CRO 3RY, England

ISBN 0 900549 97 1
First published 1986

Photoset and printed in Great Britain by
Netherwood, Dalton & Company Ltd
Bradley Mills, Huddersfield, West Yorkshire.

Contents

Introduction

Although there is an undeniable continuity of philosophy linking the Mercedes-Benz models of the 1970s to their predecessors, there were also three significant new influences on their design. Two – the increased emphasis on safety and the need to reduce environmental pollution by exhaust gases – were the result of legislative requirements, while the third – the search for greater fuel economy – was brought about by the vast increases in fuel costs during the 1970s. The story of how Stuttgart's designers succeeded in meeting these often conflicting new requirements and at the same time increased the Daimler-Benz company's technological lead over the rest of the world's motor manufacturers is, I think, a fascinating one, and it is this which I have attempted to tell in the present *Collector's Guide*.

In the 1970s lie also the roots of those design philosophies which have shaped the models of the 1980s, and so I have deliberately taken a brief look at today's models in Chapter 1 in order to show that continuity at work once again. Sadly, pressure of space has prevented me from looking more closely at the latest generation of classics from Stuttgart – the 'compact' W201s, the medium-range W124s, and the S-class W126s. Nevertheless, it would be invidious to divide the 1970s off from the 1980s completely, for the W107 SL sports cars and W123 saloons, coupes and estates have spanned both decades. The story of the later W107s, which is told in Chapter 3, is in fact an illustration in microcosm of many of the important developments made in the 1980s, for these cars have been progressively updated with the latest mechanical improvements.

This is the third volume of the *Collector's Guide* trilogy on Mercedes-Benz cars since the end of the Second World War. In many ways, it has been the most difficult of the three volumes to write, thanks in no small measure to the immense complexity of model-variations brought about by the sometimes widely-differing requirements of the European and North American markets. I hope that I have been able to introduce a degree of clarity into the confusion; what I can say for certain is that I have emerged from writing this volume with my appreciation of the cars not only intact, but actually enhanced!

Woodcote, Oxfordshire
January 1986

JAMES L. TAYLOR

S CE 7537

Acknowledgements

It would be ungentlemanly of me not to admit that my knowledge of the innermost workings of the Daimler-Benz empire in the 1970s and 1980s has been considerably increased by a regular reading of *Car* magazine, which I continue to rate as the best of its kind in the English language. For more specific information, however, I have been dependent on the generous assistance of many Mercedes-Benz enthusiasts and owners. I am indebted, too, to Messrs Karnowski and Von Pein at the Daimler-Benz historical archives in Stuttgart, and to A. B. Shuman at Mercedes-Benz of North America, for their help in providing documentation and photographs, and I confess to having drawn heavily on the vast store of material owned by my publisher, John Blunsden. The editors of *Autocar, Motor,* and *Road & Track* have once again kindly allowed me to quote from their excellent publications, and the management of Greenoaks Garages Ltd of South Croydon, Surrey, were most helpful in putting at our disposal, for photographic purposes, several cars from their abundant stock of previously used models.

Finally, my thanks go once more to my dear wife Lesley Ann, who has not only become a Mercedes-Benz enthusiast during the writing of this book, but has also contributed the cover photograph and a number of those inside.

J.L.T.

CHAPTER 1

Daimler-Benz since 1970

Expansion and advanced technology

The dominant feature of the Daimler-Benz empire in the 1970s and 1980s has been the expansion of its car division, all the more remarkable for having occurred at such a difficult time for the motor industry. While other major manufacturers have joined forces to face the new challenges, the Daimler-Benz car division has stood aloof, deigning only to seek the assistance of a specialist engineering company like Cosworth (for the 16-valve version of the 2.3-litre 190 engine) or a specialist like Steyr-Daimler-Puch (in the development and build of the G-Wagen off-road car). Outside the car division, Daimler-Benz has suffered the same setbacks as other manufacturers, with massive losses in its truck and bus division; and even on the fringes of the successful car division, the G-Wagen has failed to push the Range Rover and Toyota Land Cruiser from their pre-eminent market positions. Overall profitability has never been in doubt, however, thanks to the revenue from the cars. Thus, despite losses amounting to £920 million as a result of the German metalworkers' strike in 1984, Daimler-Benz still returned a huge profit for the financial year.

Some of the ways in which Mercedes-Benz cars survived the difficult 1970s are set out below, and the cars themselves are the subjects of the ensuing chapters; but first, it is interesting to see just how much the company has expanded. In 1970, the company's total workforce was 116,985, and by 1984 this had increased to 155,000. Car production reflects that expansion even more dramatically in an era when mechanization of production was on the increase, with 280,419 units built in 1970, 401,255 in 1977 and 476,183 in 1983. By the end of 1984, the company claimed to be equipped to build between 520,000 and 540,000 cars a year. Success in the North American market has made no small contribution to these totals, and figures of 29,108 car sales for 1970, 48,872 for 1977 and 79,222 for 1984 demonstrate how Daimler-Benz's determination to succeed in that market in the face of some of the severe difficulties discussed later in this chapter has paid off. Indeed, much of the effort which went into designing cars to suit American requirements paid handsome dividends in improvements for other markets, too, and will continue to do so now that stricter emissions laws are being introduced in Europe.

The clearest example in recent years of the car division's expansion has been the supplementing of production at the Sindelfingen works in Stuttgart by production at Bremen, in northern Germany. The Bremen factory is actually the old Borgward plant, which was used exclusively for the production of light commercials until lack of capacity at Sindelfingen forced the installation there of the assembly lines for the W123 T-series estate cars in 1978. (By 1985, the Bremen plant was completely given over to car production, building especially 190s for export markets, for which task it was ideally situated close to splendid port facilities. Indeed, but for opposition from trade unions and local government, Daimler-Benz would certainly have turned Bremen into an all-car plant even earlier, and thus production would have expanded that much more quickly.) If the 1970s taught Daimler-Benz one thing for the future, however, it was that demand can fluctuate sharply as a result of entirely unpredictable outside influences – in this case, the Energy Crisis. As a hedge against the repetition of such difficulties, production flexibility was designed-in to the new model ranges of the 1980s:

New US legislation was just beginning to bite as the 1970s began. The cars shown here are all 1972 US-market models, with emissions-controlled engines and special headlamps and bumpers. All had the then-new 4½-litre V8 engine. The SL shape had first been seen in 1971, but the 280SEL 4.5 in the background was a much older design, dating from the mid-1960s. It would be replaced later in 1972 by the new W116 S-class cars.

the W201 compact saloons and the W124 medium-sized saloons (which will be the subject of a future *Collector's Guide*) were designed to be built on the same assembly lines, so that only minor revisions of tooling would be required to change from one model to the other. In this way, the company made sure it would be able to react very quickly and cheaply to fluctuations in the market or changes in buyer preference.

The names of the key figures at Daimler-Benz during the 1970s and early 1980s will occur over and over again in this book, and it is worthwhile putting them into context before going any further. Responsible more than any other for the expansion of the car division was Joachim Zahn, Chairman of the Board from 1966 until 1979 and a career finance expert. He was succeeded at the helm by the company's former Chief Buyer, Gerhard Prinz. But Prinz, a lawyer by training, died suddenly in 1983, and his place was taken by an engineer, Werner Breitschwerdt, who had joined

Outside the scope of this book, but related to the cars by certain common mechanical components, is the four-wheel-drive Geländewagen, familiarly known as the G-Wagen. Pictured here is a right-hand-drive, long-wheelbase model. Daimler-Benz, of course, is also Germany's largest manufacturer of commercial vehicles.

the company in 1953 and had risen to become Director of Research.

An even more direct influence on the company's cars has been exerted by its leading engineers, of course, many of whom have made their whole careers with Daimler-Benz. The responsibility for uniting the work of the various departments into whole cars rests with the Chief Engineer, and it is particularly noticeable how the modern Mercedes-Benz *is* a whole car, and not just an assembly of disparate ideas. The principal architect of this approach was Hans Scherenberg, Chief Engineer from 1965 to 1977, and his work has been ably carried on by the present occupant of the hottest seat on the Daimler-Benz Board, Friedrich van Winsen. After Rudolf Uhlenhaut retired as Research Director in 1972, engineering research was placed in the hands of Erich Waxenberger until Werner Breitschwerdt took over in 1977. On his elevation to the Chairmanship in 1983, Rudolf Hörning succeeded to the research post. Until 1973, styling remained in the hands of Karl Wilfert, who had had overall responsibility for the shapes of the 1960s, but the cars of the 1980s have been mainly styled by Italian-born Bruno Sacco, a Wilfert protégé who has been with the company since the late 1950s and who took charge of Daimler-Benz styling in 1975. Finally, most of the significant engine developments affecting the cars of the 1980s, including the later SL models featured in Chapter 3, have been carried out by teams working under Kurt Oblander.

It would be easy to imagine that men like these have been solely responsible for the creation of the modern Mercedes-Benz; but it is not so, and indeed they have had to contend with increasingly restrictive outside influences since the 1970s which have shaped

Prof Dr Hans Scherenberg, Chief Engineer from 1965 to 1977, was mainly responsible for the engineering effort behind the 1970s models.

Head of Research at Stuttgart in the late 1970s, and latterly Chairman of the Board of Directors, was Professor Werner Breitschwerdt.

Successor to Breitschwerdt, first as Research Director and then as Chairman, was Dr Rudolf Hörnig.

the cars just as much. It was in the 1960s that legislation first began to have a serious effect on automotive design, when the US Government reacted to Ralph Nader's vindictive and exaggerated crusade against the Chevrolet Corvair by introducing a set of legally-enforceable safety standards for new cars sold in the USA. These regulations were followed a few years later in that country by another set which limited the amounts of noxious gases (principally carbon monoxide and oxides of nitrogen) permissible in vehicle exhausts. The Americans had a point – thousands of their citizens were suffering death or serious injury on the roads every year thanks to the thoughtless design of some of their cars (mainly the home-grown product, in fact), and the cities of the West Coast were becoming smog-zones as a result of both industrial pollution and the exhaust fumes of the high motor-vehicle population (again the home-grown cars with their huge and inefficient engines were mainly to blame). Any manufacturer who wanted to sell cars in the USA – and Daimler-Benz most certainly did – had to comply with the new rules, and so began the era of the safety-car and exhaust-emissions controls.

Before long, other countries decided to follow the American lead, although their legislation was rarely as tough as that in the USA. The exhaust emissions rules in America, first applied to new cars in 1968, were gradually toughened in a series of steps over the next few years. The details of these regulations are of little interest, but their effect was to smother engine performance, to remove some of the refinement so carefully designed-in at Stuttgart, and to increase fuel consumption to levels which would have been unacceptable in Europe. The Americans, used to cheap petrol and the atrocious fuel-efficiency of some of their own cars, accepted the compromise with scarcely a murmur, but Daimler-Benz recognized that they could not risk their reputation by selling these Americanized vehicles in Europe. As a result, they were obliged to build very different versions of their cars for the two markets.

As if this was not enough, the real blow struck in 1973, when the Arab-Israeli War put an end to cheap oil supplies to the Western world, and all of a sudden Daimler-Benz found themselves with cars which had put on weight to meet new safety legislation, and which drank fuel at an alarming rate thanks to this extra weight and to their exhaust-emissions control gear. All this was at a time when petrol prices seemed certain to go up and up,

Essential to the expansion of car production in the 1980s was the Bremen plant, at which the W123 estates had been built since the end of 1977.

as indeed they have done ever since 1973. The problem was perhaps less acute outside the USA because only that country insisted on the extra weight of additional safety equipment, the full fuel-squandering emissions-control gear, and inefficient low-octane lead-free gasoline; but it was immediately clear to Stuttgart's engineers that they had to take drastic action. Henceforth, the accent would be on weight-saving, and on fuel-saving measures such as more efficient engines and higher gearing. That they responded so whole-heartedly to the problems raised by the Energy Crisis of the 1970s undoubtedly helped to put them in the forefront of the technological revolution which was forced upon car manufacturers in the late 1970s and early 1980s. Any news of forthcoming Daimler-Benz technology is now avidly seized upon by other manufacturers as an indication of future trends in car design.

All this makes it sound easy, which it most certainly was not. In the USA, what saved Daimler-Benz was their range of diesel models. As America swung heavily towards diesel power, which offered greater fuel economy at the expense of performance, so Stuttgart exported more and more diesel cars to meet the

The major plant was nevertheless still at Sindelfingen, in Stuttgart. Here some of the last W123 saloons and an early W201 compact model come off the lines side by side.

demand, and by the mid-1970s they had special, US-market only, diesel models ready to be launched. In Europe, where diesel power is still largely associated with taxis and commercial vehicles, who would have bought a diesel edition of the W123 medium-range coupe, or of the W116 S-class flagship saloons? The Americans did, in droves, and Stuttgart developed turbo-charged versions of their diesel engines specially for them.

It was probably the diesel models, too, which enabled Daimler-Benz to continue exporting some of their larger petrol-engined cars to the USA at all. Regardless of the great strides made by the company's engineers in improving fuel economy, the big Mercedes-Benz models have never exactly been frugal users of fuel, and once the CAFE (Corporate Average Fuel Economy) rules had been introduced in the USA, their number would surely have been up but for the balancing effect of the diesel cars. Under the CAFE rules, manufacturers are allowed to sell thirsty cars on condition that the average fuel economy of *all* the cars they sell reaches a certain standard, so that large sales of an economy model will offset low-volume sales of a bigger-engined car. Those who do not comply are subject to a system of fines – which Daimler-Benz have never yet been obliged to pay.

All this development effort has been vindicated by more recent developments in Europe, of course, where the West German Government has led a campaign to legislate for cleaner exhausts throughout the EEC. From January 1, 1989, common standards relating to noxious emissions and the use of lead-free fuel will apply throughout the Community, but in the meantime, West Germany has decided to make an early start by introducing a system of tax exemptions for new cars fitted with 'clean' exhausts after January 1, 1986. In conjunction with the use of catalytic converters similar to those developed for the American market in the later 1970s, Daimler-Benz has decided to fit all its European petrol-engined cars with a new MF (multi-function) system by which fuel mixture and ignition settings can be adjusted easily to suit requirements. Thus, only a simple service adjustment is required to change from leaded to lead-free fuel, or from premium to regular-grade petrol of either type, and West German customers can choose whether to buy their new car ready fitted with the catalytic converter and tuned for lead-free fuel (in which case they will benefit by tax exemption), or to wait until 1989 before fitting the catalytic converter and running until then on leaded petrol. One obvious benefit to Daimler-Benz will be that Federal and European versions of their cars will no longer have to be quite so different.

If fuel economy and exhaust emissions-control legislation caused Stuttgart's biggest headaches in the 1970s and early 1980s, safety regulations certainly came a close second. In the 1960s, when the new rules first appeared in America, existing Mercedes-Benz models already met or exceeded almost all the new safety criteria: after all, the company had been one of the pioneers of automotive safety in the previous decade. Yet, like the emissions-control regulations, those governing safety in the US car market gradually tightened. By the early 1970s, new cars had to be subjected to a series of crash tests (admirable in principle but often unrealistic in practice) before they could even be admitted to the USA, and the only way to get cars through some of the tests was by reinforcing their body structures. Generally speaking, this meant adding weight, which ran directly contrary in later years to the requirement for better fuel economy. The new Mercedes-Benz cars of the early 1970s were built like tanks as a consequence of the new safety rules, and the 1973 American requirement for impact-absorbing bumpers did nothing for what was already ponderous styling. It was not until the very end of the 1970s that the deformable bumpers of the W126 S-class cars showed how to meet the rules – a 5mph frontal impact and 2½mph rear impact without damage to safety-related equipment, such as lights – without also doing violence to the stylist's visions.

As acknowledged leaders in automotive safety before the onset of the new regulations, Daimler-Benz would no doubt have felt obliged to participate in the safety-research programme promoted by the US Government's Department of Transportation in the early 1970s, even if an agreement between the West German and US Governments had not forced their hand. The idea was that a series of conferences would be held, at intervals of 9-10 months, at which the participating manufacturers would compare notes on progress. Given the motor industry's natural reluctance to reveal significant developments to rival manufacturers and its similar tendency to score points off them whenever possible, the concept could never have been other than a recipe for disaster. Nevertheless, five such conferences were held between May 1971 and June 1974. What these revealed more than anything else was that the aims of the DoT's scheme to develop the ideal ESV (Experimental Safety Vehicle) were ill-defined and in some cases impracticable. Although the DoT promised a re-orientation of the programme, its best intentions became bogged-down in American bureaucracy. 'Lacking any formal changes in the programme,' Hans Scherenberg was later to say, 'we decided to establish our own project concept.' Daimler-Benz were not alone in this and, when the DoT found itself unable to unite the participating manufacturers to work towards a common goal, the ESV scheme collapsed.

Nevertheless, it had led to the building of some intriguing prototypes at Stuttgart. Known as ESFs (Experimental-Sicherheits-Fahrzeug, which is German for ESV), five were shown at the various ESV conferences. ESF-03 was the first, and was presented at the 1971 Paris conference. Based on a W114 mid-range saloon, it was modified to protect its occupants in a 50mph frontal barrier impact and a 15mph side impact. Daimler-Benz themselves hosted the second conference later that year at Sindelfingen, where they presented ESF-05, still based on a New Generation saloon, but featuring a redesigned front end, plus even bigger and more ridiculous-looking bumpers than ESF-03. This car was designed to enable its occupants to survive an even wider variety of severe impacts than its predecessor. The Washington conference in May 1972 then saw ESF-13, based on a W108 S-class car with altered front and rear details, and designed to show that the requirements met in ESF-05 could be satisfied in a more aesthetically pleasing manner. In order to increase the length of the crushable front zone, this car was fitted with a special 'short' engine, a 140bhp V6 of 2.8 litres, developed from the production V8 unit.

It was with ESF-22, based on a 450SE saloon and shown to the spring 1973 conference in Kyoto, Japan, that Daimler-Benz demonstrated their intention to go their own way. Whereas the ESV programme's goal had been occupant survival after a 50mph barrier impact, Stuttgart's engineers argued that accident research questioned the need to attain such standards, the meeting of which therefore added both cost and weight to a car unnecessarily. Their own researches showed the need for a car which would protect its occupants in a barrier crash at no more than 40mph, and at the same speed in an oblique impact with a moving barrier, which more closely approximated to the most common type of vehicle collision. Also at variance with the DoT's programme was Daimler-Benz's emphasis on 'active' restraints – in this case three-point inertia-reel safety-belts on all seats. The driver of ESF-22 was further protected by an air-bag stowed in the steering-wheel hub, which automatically inflated to act as a cushion in a frontal collision. Unfortunately the car suffered the usual weight penalty. It was 465lb heavier than a production 450SE and would have needed further weight increases of up to 140lb to provide the durability necessary in a production car. Stuttgart thought that such weight increases were unacceptable at a time when fuel conservation was on the agenda, and told the Kyoto conference so. Moreover, they considered that mass production of such a car was not economically feasible.

The last ESF was ESF-24, shown at the London conference in 1974, and in essence it was a production 450SE. Where the production car met 30mph frontal collision criteria, the ESF would withstand a 40mph frontal barrier impact, and in addition it had an experimental anti-lock braking system and fatter tyres. The penalty was a 10% increase in weight. Stuttgart had made its point: the production W116 was already 'safe' enough in most departments, and improvements were already in hand for future production cars. A vehicle did not have to look like a mobile fortress to protect its occupants, and moreover, the DoT's programme ignored the fact that more than half the safety battle was *preventing* accidents. The W116 already showed, as would

Safety has been a major preoccupation at Stuttgart ever since Daimler-Benz built its first safety vehicle in the 1930s. ESF 13 was one of several Mercedes-Benz Experimental Safety Vehicles produced in the early 1970s to meet crash-resistance standards proposed by the US Department of Transportation. It was shown at the Transpo 72 exhibition in Washington in May 1972, was based on the current W108 S-class saloon (covered in volume 2 of this series) and powered by a 140bhp 2.8-litre V6 engine.

the cars of the later 1970s, how Daimler-Benz were concentrating on removing driver stress as the major means to this end.

The ESV conferences turned a spotlight on to Stuttgart's safety-related research, but the fact is that such research goes on all the time. The anti-lock brakes seen on ESF-24 and made available as an optional extra on production models in 1980 had first been demonstrated in 1970, before the ESV programme began. Developed in conjunction with Telefunken, in Germany, the original Teldix system was superseded before production commenced by one developed with Bosch. This system, known as ABS, or 'Anti-Blockier-System', has probably been the greatest single contribution to automotive safety in recent years, and has been widely copied. With it, a car can be safely steered on a wet road under heavy braking as sensors on each wheel momentarily release that wheel's brake just before the wheel locks and causes a skid. The air-bags seen during the ESV programme have also gone into production and, more recently still, an automatic locking differential, a wheelspin control system and an automatically-engaged four-wheel-drive system have been developed to give the modern Mercedes-Benz the widest selection of aids to traction – and therefore to safety as well – available anywhere in the world.

Such research costs a great deal of money, as Daimler-Benz are not loath to admit. One 1984 advertisement for the W123 saloons boasted that 'Mercedes-Benz spend over a million pounds a day, seven days a week, on research and development in areas related to safety, environmental factors, noise-reduction and greater efficiency, as well as the very latest advances in electronic and mechanical automotive technology'. Not surprisingly, it is the customer who funds that research. Mercedes-Benz cars have never been cheap, even in their native Germany (prices elsewhere are often artificially inflated by import duties and the like), and it has always been the company's practice to offer its products with very low levels of equipment in order to keep the base-price

The C-111 experimental car, first seen in 1969 as a testbed for the Wankel rotary engine, ran at the Nardo track twice during the 1970s. In 1976, it was fitted with much-modified bodywork and a turbocharged diesel engine to set new speed records in its class; it is pictured here on its re-appearance in 1979, when it took five more world records, this time powered by a 500bhp twin-turbo-charged V8 petrol engine.

The 450SLC 5.0 enjoyed a brief rally career, and was first seen in the Rally of Portugal in March 1979. Björn Waldegaard drove the car pictured here, which formed part of the first Daimler-Benz works rally team to enter a European event for 17 years.

Although Daimler-Benz failed to live up to their past competitions reputation, Mikkola and Hertz did drive this 450SLC 5.0 to victory in the 1979 Bandama Rally.

down, in the knowledge that most customers would then be tempted to spend quite a lot extra on items from the extensive options list.

The enormous cost of research has almost certainly been one of the reasons why the company has not participated openly in motor sport in the 1970s and early 1980s; probably image considerations have done the rest, for Daimler-Benz's past successes have been such that to fail publicly would damage the mystique left by past glories. Nevertheless, the factory's competitions department has prepared cars for allegedly private entrants in motor sport, and in the late 1970s, 450SLCs, 450SLC 5.0s and 280Es were among the cars which entered competitions with such thinly-disguised factory support. Despite a number of successes, however – including a 280E in first place and three others among the first 10 finishers in the 1978 London-to-Sydney Marathon – Daimler-Benz never put up a proper works team. Probably the nearest they came to it was in 1980, when a plan to enter rallying had a fair wind for a while. World Champion Walter Röhrl was even signed-up as the number-one works driver, but the Board axed the project before the year was out. Later on, a plan to enter Group B rallies with a 16-valve version of the W201 190 saloon met the same fate, and all that remained was the idea for a 16-valve 190, which would resurface in rather tamer form as the production 190E 2.3-16 of 1984. Unexplained at the time of writing, though, is a three-door VW Golf-sized hatchback seen on test at the company's Untertürkheim proving-ground in mid-1981 by Germany's *Auto-Zeitung* magazine, and which an embarrassed Daimler-Benz described as a rally car prototype after photographs had been published. From the B-pillars forward it was pure W201, while the rear 'hatch' was W123 estate and the rear body was fabricated. It was certainly too wasteful of space to be a super-mini of some kind – but if it really *was* a rally car prototype, what has happened to the rally car?

Throughout the 1970s and early 1980s, Daimler-Benz has managed to retain that image of solid conservatism which it gained in the two previous decades. There has been, for example, neither front-wheel-drive car (though prototypes were built for the W201), nor hatchback saloon (except for the Auto 2000 car). Four-wheel drive has only very recently come into the picture. Yet the company has persistently led the field in the area of automotive technology. It is a curious contradiction, but one with which the company is happy to live because this conservatism is important to many of its customers. Presumably these customers turn a blind eye to such well-publicized events as the re-activation of the experimental C-111 in 1976 to take several world speed records with its turbocharged diesel engine, or to the Auto 2000 concept-car built in response to a project sponsored by the West German Ministry of Research and Technology. This project divided a £33 million grant among Volkswagen, Audi, Daimler-Benz and a team of automotive engineers from various German universities, in an attempt to encourage the development of a realistic car of the future. Stuttgart based its prototype on a W126 S-class car in order to demonstrate its conviction that the big car still had a future in a world concerned with energy conservation. Extensive use of alloys parallelled current mainstream development work, as did noise insulation through the use of a capsule around the engine. A computer-controlled four-speed automatic gearbox, with selectable 'Fast', 'Economy', or 'City' settings, also revealed something Daimler-Benz had in mind for early introduction, but the ugly styling of the car, with its blunt Kamm tail and hatchback, was probably misleading to those seeking clues to the shape of future Mercedes. The engine options, however, were a fascinating insight into the future, for they were a 3.8-litre petrol V8 with a cylinder cut-out mechanism, a 3.3-litre twin-turbo V6 diesel, and a 126bhp gas turbine which by the time the car was seen at the 1981 Frankfurt Show had only been bench-tested. Both petrol and diesel units were expected to push the car above 125mph, and to offer fuel economy in the 35-40mpg range. Work on the gas turbine engine was still continuing during 1985. If that kind of thing is conservative, perhaps dictionary definitions of the word need to be amended . . . . .

In any case, for those who wanted all the high-technology of a modern Mercedes-Benz without the conservative image, a solution was already to hand. Partly, it had been brought about by the high volumes in which Stuttgart now produced even its more prestigious models, because there are always customers who want their cars to look different from the other thousand of the same type produced that day or that week; no doubt a sociologist would say it had come about as the reaction of individuals to the increasing volume of restrictive legislation being applied to the car and its driver. The solution was customizing, or 'personalizing' as some specialists prefer to call it.

Customizing had really originated in America in the late 1950s as an echo of the 'dream cars' then proliferating on the show stands of the big manufacturers. The difference, though, was that in the late 1970s the perpetrators were the very rich and the subjects were brand-new Mercedes-Benz and other prestigious cars rather than worn-out American bangers. Its essence, as applied in such cases, was the addition of an uprated engine and chassis, plus as much cosmetic alteration of interior and bodywork as the customer wanted or could afford. Or, indeed, the customer might just settle for the cosmetics without the tuning. Favourites in the Mercedes-Benz range for the treatment have been the W201s, with the W126 saloons and coupes lagging some way behind and the W107 roadsters and W123 saloons and coupes being converted in smaller but still significant numbers. A few conversions have also been carried out on the W116 S-class saloons.

Although the W126 S-class saloons, which replaced the W116 range, were not widely available until 1980, they were most definitely a 1970s design and were first seen at Frankfurt in 1979. Improved aerodynamics and lighter weight helped to make them 10% more fuel-efficient than the earlier models.

To be frank, some of the customized Mercedes-Benz cars which have appeared in recent years have been of the most appalling vulgarity. Stuttgart in fact forbids the builders of the most garish examples (usually for the Arab market, although Germany and the USA are also persistent offenders) to leave the three-pointed star on the vehicles, but it does give tacit approval to a small number of the more reputable firms. These include the most famous Mercedes-Benz converters – AMG, of Affalterbach, just outside Stuttgart itself. The company is run by Hans-Werner Aufrecht, a former Daimler-Benz development engineer who started in a small way tuning Mercedes-Benz cars in 1967, and has never looked back since he started doing custom bodywork for them 11 years later. One of his best pieces of work is still mechanical, however, and that is his four-cam version of the 5-litre V8 engine, with 340bhp on tap. Other well-known makers of bolt-on styling addenda include Lorinser and Kamei, but many other coachbuilding firms have also been commissioned to customize Mercedes-Benz cars for the rich. Among the most outlandish conversions have been by Styling Garage (SGS) in Hamburg, and by the Swiss Franco Sbarro, both of whom have turned W126 SEC models into gullwinged monsters. Most subtle of all, perhaps, has been another Swiss, Peter Monteverdi, who simply rebuilds S-class saloons to his own specification, kits them out with refinements to suit his wealthy customers, and sells them not as Mercedes-Benzes, but as Monteverdis.

The 1980s and beyond

Finally, what does the future hold for Mercedes-Benz cars? Even more advanced technology, without a doubt. Greater production volumes, too, perhaps with more emphasis on the smaller models and on diesel variants, although Stuttgart is convinced that the big car will not die. Drivers can expect future Mercedes-Benz models to be even more pleasant to drive, thanks to experiments conducted at the company's £6.6 million advanced simulator in West Berlin, unveiled in early 1985. More specifically, 1986 will probably see the arrival of a replacement SL model, allegedly called R129 and based on the W201 shape. The W126 S-class will fall due for replacement in 1988, and work is already under way on its W140 successor. There will be new engines aplenty, both smaller and bigger than existing units, but with the emphasis firmly on fuel economy and 'clean' exhausts without loss of performance. Since 1980, Daimler-Benz has also been one of a number of manufacturers investigating the possibilities of a dashboard-mounted electronic road map which selects the driver's route for him. When the time comes to prepare a fourth volume of this *Collector's Guide* series there should be a great deal of interesting developments to record.

CHAPTER 2

Sports cars and coupes

The SL and SLC models

The earliest traces of the W107 project date back to November 1967, when it was considered simply as a direct replacement for the W113 SL two-seater models introduced in 1963, and it was some time later that the idea of the SLC model to replace the ageing W111 two-door coupes was grafted on to the project. From that point forward, though, the SL and SLC designs proceeded in tandem. Both grew up in the climate of the late 1960s, when motor manufacturers were striving to come to grips with the new American legislation which obliged them to build cars which protected their occupants to a high standard in an acccident, and which emitted fewer noxious gases through their exhaust pipes. Stuttgart's anxiety to continue selling cars in the USA, which at that time took rather less than 15% of all Mercedes-Benz cars built, forced them to comply with the new rules, and thus the SL and SLC W107s became the first Mercedes-Benz models designed around the requirements of the North American market. Even 1954's 300SL, aimed squarely at America, had been adapted from an existing design.

The best way of making a car safer in an accident is to make it stronger, and as technology stood in the late 1960s, that entailed making it heavier. So if its performance was to equal or better that of the model it replaced, it was bound to need a more powerful engine. So it was that the W107 models were planned around the 3½-litre V8 engine which would first be seen in 1969 in the limited-volume W111 coupes and cabriolets: this engine was a full 700cc larger in displacement than the OHC 'six' which powered the outgoing W113 280SL.

The 3½-litre V8 engine has been fully described in Volume 2 of this series of *Collector's Guides*. Suffice it to reiterate here that it was a cast-iron OHC pushrod engine fed by Bosch electronic fuel injection and putting out 200bhp at 5,800rpm and 211lb/ft of torque at 4,000rpm in European form. Despite the greater weight of the W107 350SL as compared to the 280SL it replaced, the newer car was able to cover the 0-60mph dash in the same 9.3 seconds and to surge on to a maximum speed of 127mph, 6mph more than the older car could manage. The slightly heavier 350SLC was almost as quick, which gave it, too, a performance advantage over its predecessor. Four-speed synchromesh transmission was standard in both models, but the optional four-speed automatic with fluid coupling scarcely blunted the edge of this very respectable if not quite supercar performance.

Mercedes-Benz sports models had traditionally used the running gear of established saloons, and the W107s were to be no exception. The most sophisticated suspension system available 'off the shelf' (the complex and expensive air suspension system of the big 600 limousine excepted) was that introduced on the New Generation medium-sized saloons in the autumn of 1967. At the front, this differed little from previous practice except that careful angling of the unequal-length wishbones provided for a degree of anti-dive; the coil springs and telescopic shock absorbers were long-standing Mercedes-Benz features. The rear suspension, however, was by semi-trailing arms which promotional literature would always describe as 'diagonal swing-axles', as Stuttgart's policy was never to accept that there had been anything less than ideal about the infamous swing-axles which they had employed for more than three decades, and thanks to which many a surprised driver had found himself pointing the wrong way after enthusiastic cornering in the wet!

This rare high-angle photograph shows to advantage the elegant lines of an early 350SL. Note the neat metal cover for the convertible top.

Coil springs and telescopic shock absorbers were found again here, but the anti-roll bar fitted as standard to the front of the W107 was only optional at the rear.

A further optional fitment at the rear was a limited-slip differential. Tracks front and rear were identical to those of the New Generation saloons, while steering and brakes were also saloon-based, the former having power assistance as standard on the W107 to overcome the extra drag of its fatter 70-section tyres, and the latter being solid discs at the rear, but ventilated at the front to assist braking from the W107's higher speeds. As on the saloons, both servo assistance and a dual hydraulic circuit were standard.

All this gave the new cars much better handling than the old 280SL and 280SE 3.5 with their swing-axles had enjoyed, but it was still possible to overdo things in a two-seater W107 by lifting off in mid-corner, when the back of the car could let go and give the inexperienced driver a hard time; this was less likely to happen in the SLC variants, where the longer wheelbase made for greater cornering stability. It would be too easy, however, to overstate the W107's handling deficiencies; the real point was that both SL and SLC had very high levels of tolerance, so that it was most unlikely that any driver other than a road-tester trying to find the limits of the cars' handling would in fact get into trouble.

Not for nothing had the W107 been given the nickname of 'der Panzerwagen' during its development at Stuttgart; the word means tank or armoured car, and everything about the new models testified to the aptness of this description. The bodyshell construction followed familiar Mercedes-Benz 'safety cell' principles, with front and rear crumple zones, but these had been made even stronger than in earlier cars bearing the three-pointed star in order to exceed the new American crash-safety requirements. Where the old SL (though not the W111 coupes which the SLC replaced) had used some alloy panels in order to save weight, the W107 was all-steel. To meet safety legislation about side-swipe accidents, the cars' doors were of massive and bulbous construction (which Stuttgart preferred to the heavy internal reinforcement bars used by Detroit manufacturers), and their exterior handles had no push-button, but were operated by pulling, thus reducing the risk of a door opening in a side-impact accident. Maximum rollover protection from minimal thickness was provided by computer-designed windscreen pillars, which also incorporated rain channels to deflect water away from the screen and up over the roof.

The styling was just as tank-like, and the W107 in two-seater SL form had none of the lightness of the old W113. Squat and angular, it looked instead as if it had been hewn by teams of dedicated Teutonic craftsmen from a block of solid stone. In long-wheelbase SLC form, however, the styling was altogether more successful, and the SL had undoubtedly suffered more

A 350SL with its soft top erect. The ribbing along the lower edges of the body was designed to keep the upper body free of road dirt.

An early right-hand-drive car. The wipers were not altered from their left-hand-drive position.

from Stuttgart's decision to develop the two models in parallel than had the SLC. The SLC, of course, was a very different kind of car from the old W111 coupe, and its styling could not really be directly compared with that of the model it replaced. On the other hand, Karl Wilfert's stylists had stuck for the SL with the same overall size and layout as the W113s had enjoyed, adding a little width to allow for the fatter doors and a little length to make room for an optional built-in air conditioning system at the front and a token rear seat inside. As before, the SL came with a choice of soft or hard top, or both, and there was even an attempted visual link with the old 'pagoda roof' detachable hardtop of the W113, although the W107 item was not dished in the centre in the same way, but merely bore twin bright strips to deflect rain in the same idiom as the W114 New Generation coupes. One link certainly was not broken, however, for the massive hardtop was every bit as heavy as the older car's, and still needed two people to manhandle it into position!

Generally, though, W107 styling was all-new, and in essence the cars had a gentle wedge-shape, with their boot-lids higher than the bonnet-line. The wide 'sports' type Mercedes-Benz grille was flanked by rectangular horizontal headlights with wraparound indicator lamps which featured ribbed lenses to help keep them clean. The rear light clusters were also ribbed, and massive in size compared to those of the superseded W111s and W113s. The ribbing theme was continued along the lower body sides below the rubbing strip, which visually linked the wraparound front and rear bumpers, and was designed primarily to deflect water and dirt thrown up by the road wheels and thus to keep the body sides and windows clean. Fortuitously or not, it also combined with a blacked-out sill panel to slim the appearance of what was actually a fairly tall and bulky body in two-seater form.

That tallness and bulkiness were both smoothed out by the extra 14.1 inches in the wheelbase of the SLC models, however.

A dramatic low-angle picture of an early car, clearly showing the foglamps fitted as standard below the front bumper.

These cars, of which no open version was ever planned on account of fears that the body strengthening necessary would render them too heavy, shared their sheet metal with the SL up to window-height apart from the extra length in the wheelbase behind the doors to give room for a proper rear seat. However, the completely different fixed roof of the SLC made it 1.8 inches taller than the two-seater model. The side window treatment tended to polarize opinions of the styling when the cars were new,

The twin-barrelled exhaust and squat stance contributed to the high-performance image. This is a 450SL, as the badging clearly shows. Note the 'pagoda roof' effect carried over from the previous SL series.

for Wilfert's team had settled for a fixed louvre arrangement at the rearmost edge of the coupe roof. The reason was quite straightforward. Mercedes-Benz coupe tradition demanded that all the side windows wind down out of sight for fine-weather motoring, and in the SLC this was not possible because the trailing edge of the rear side window was directly above the wheelarch. To have specified one opening window and one fixed one would have looked even odder, so the louvres were chosen as an attractive compromise – or an unattractive one, depending on individual taste.

Interior arrangements from the B-pillars forward were identical for both cars. Firm, supportive seats covered in cloth, or optionally in leather, were fitted with adjustable headrests and enjoyed a whole range of rake and height adjustment. Noteworthy was the way in which the seat backs pivoted about 6 inches above the seat cushion, so that as the backrest rake was altered, so the degree of lumbar support also changed. For the first few months of production, inertia-reel seat belts were optional, but were soon standardized.

Once settled behind the large four-spoke 'safety' steering-wheel which made its first appearance in the 350SL, the driver was faced by a well-arranged display of three circular instruments beneath glass angled to inhibit glare in a cowl rising gently out of the moulded-plastic dashboard. Below these, a

The appearance of the interior in this shot of a 350SL shows why the model was more of a two-seater luxury tourer than a traditional sports car. The general air of massive solidity was typical of Stuttgart's designs at this time.

battery of warning lights was arranged in a horizontal strip, while the column bore the familiar Mercedes-Benz multi-function stalk to operate indicators and wash-wipe. A centre console divided the front of the passenger space into two distinct compartments, and held the radio and various minor controls. Here lay the only jarring note, for cars equipped with air conditioning (as were all US models) had an extraordinarily untidy array of knobs and switches on the console's 'climate control panel', which resembled nothing so much as a test engineer's auxiliary instrument lash-up. The air conditioning system operated through the same dashboard vents as the heating and ventilation system, which followed standard Mercedes-Benz practice in offering separate controls for driver and passenger. A new feature, though, was ducting in the doors, thus providing all-round warmth or cool air according to choice.

Left-hand-drive models followed American fashion with a foot-operated parking brake, but right-hand-drive cars had a proper handbrake mounted on the transmission tunnel. All variants with automatic transmission had the same centrally-mounted selector with its much-praised dog's leg gate, while manual-gearbox cars had a nicely shaped shift lever sited, once again, on the transmission tunnel. There were pleasant little touches, too, like the remote-control door mirror operated manually from inside the car, and a detachable map-reading/emergency light in the glove box which was on permanent trickle-charge when not in use. All the instruments and controls had a pleasant solidity to them, which reinforced the strong impression given by the road behaviour of a heavy, but agile, car.

Behind the B-pillars, of course, the extra inches in the SLC's wheelbase made themselves felt. Instead of the padded luggage space, which in the SL could be optionally filled by token rear seats suitable for young (and not claustrophobic) children, the larger car had a genuine rear seat for two and legroom which, if not exactly generous, was certainly adequate. Tall passengers might quarrel with the low rear roof-line, but this was a real four-seater car and not an overpriced 2 + 2, and to prove that they really meant four adults to use it, Stuttgart had extended the boot forward into the space occupied on an SL by the hood-well. This put luggage space up to 9.9cu ft, which may not be spectacular by later standards, but was well up to the facilities offered by many contemporary four-seater family cars. A final neat touch for the SLC was the provision in the rear parcel shelf of a hinged flap, beneath which nestled a small first-aid kit.

Such levels of equipment were only to be expected on a luxury coupe like the SLC, perhaps, but they turned the SL into less of a sports car than a luxury two-seat Grand Tourer. Yet this was the way Daimler-Benz had interpreted the term 'sports car' since the early 1960s. By now, it was expected of them – and the customers certainly did not complain, for the short-wheelbase W107 was an instant sales success. The prices of both SL and SLC reflected their market alignment with the expensive S-class saloons, but Daimler-Benz rapidly found they could hardly make enough to satisfy demand.

American models and the 350SL 4.5

The 350SL was launched on the European market on April 17,

This shot of a 350SL's engine bay clearly shows how the massive pancake air cleaner was made to nestle between the two cam covers in order to retain a smooth bonnet line.

The cockpit and facia of a 350SL—neat and functional, like all Stuttgart's designs for the 1970s.

1971, and the 350SLC followed about 10 months later after first being seen at the October 1971 Paris Show. For the USA, however, things were slightly different. For 1972, stricter emissions-control regulations were due to be enforced, and there was no way in which the 3½-litre engine could be made to meet those regulations without unacceptable power losses. So, right from their introduction in July 1971, W107 SLs for the American market were fitted with the new M117 4½-litre V8 engine which went at the same time into the mid-range W108/109 saloons; the roadster was known as a 350SL 4.5, although it bore ordinary 350SL badging, but the long-wheelbase car which arrived later was always a 350SLC, both in sales literature and in badging. No explanation of this curious anomaly seems to be available!

Right from the beginning, US-market W107s differed visually from their European counterparts, having twin round headlamps flanked by the standard wraparound indicator lenses which covered running lights, while the indicators were faired neatly into the valance below the front bumper. For 1972, the changes became more marked as the cars sprouted extended bumpers front and rear to meet the new American impact legislation. These bumpers bore large rubber overriders and, together with their tough mounting brackets, added considerably to the overall weight of the cars.

The 4½-litre V8 engine was not totally new, of course, but rather a long-stroke variant of the M116 3½-litre V8. That longer stroke, however, involved a taller cylinder block as well as a new crankshaft; and the M117's cylinder heads had enlarged combustion chambers to combat the power-sapping effects of a compression ratio lowered to 8:1. The latter was necessary because the fuel and ignition settings needed to keep hydrocarbon and carbon monoxide emissions within the regulations raised combustion temperatures and nitrous oxide emissions, and the only way to keep these latter emissions within the law was to lower the compression ratio. In addition, the new engine anticipated forthcoming American legislation by being designed to run on unleaded fuel. A telling indicator of the effects 1972's exhaust-emissions regulations had on the internal combustion engine was that the Federal 4½-litre V8 produced only 195bhp – 5bhp less than the non-detoxed V8 with a whole litre less capacity – and the later Californian version with its additional catalytic convertors in the exhaust system put out even less! Certainly, maximum bhp was developed at a more relaxed crankshaft speed, but bigger engines inevitably used more fuel in those days and Mercedes-Benz admitted to a 10% increase in fuel consumption for the 4½-litre cars despite the 'economy' rear axle ratio of 3.07:1 (as compared to the 3.46:1 of European 3½-litre models) which the 4½-litre engine's increased torque permitted. This meant that a Californian SL two-seater was guzzling gasoline at roughly the same rate as a Rolls-Royce Silver Shadow!

With the 4½-litre V8, the only transmission available was an all-new three-speed automatic with torque converter. Some reports at the time suggested that Stuttgart simply did not have another gearbox available which was man enough for the 279lb/ft torque of the Federal 4½-litre engine, but the real explanation can again be traced to the effects of American legislation. Each new power-train had to go through an expensive and time-consuming series of certification tests, and to offer a manual gearbox with the 4½-litre engine Stuttgart would have had to submit the W107s to an additional set of tests, and possibly even produce a version with different ignition and fuel settings to stay within the law. As some 70% of SL buyers in the USA had gone for automatic transmission in the days of the W113, there seemed little point in wasting time and money getting a manual-transmission power-train with the M117 engine certificated. So all the American-market 4½-litres had the new three-speed automatic.

Not that this was a bad thing. It offered a good degree of manual override control for the enthusiastic driver, and if used in fully-automatic mode it provided extremely smooth changes which were a major improvement over those given by the older four-speed automatic with Mercedes' fluid coupling. Inevitably, performance suffered a little, but a 350SL 4.5 could achieve 124mph, which was not far short of the 127mph claimed for the manual-transmission 350SL to European specification. So convinced were Daimler-Benz engineers of their new transmission's virtues, in fact, that they fitted it to European 350SL and 350SLC models as well after July 1972.

1973: The 450SL and 450SLC

As a model name, 350SL 4.5 did not last long, for Daimler-Benz introduced the 4½-litre engine in non-detoxed form into their European range at the Geneva Show in 1973 and the US model names were changed to parallel the new European ones. The

This side view emphasizes the longer wheelbase of the SLC compared with the SL. The louvres at the trailing edge of the rear side windows restrict the view into the rear compartment, yet allow reasonable three-quarter vision from inside the car.

350SL 4.5 thus became a 450SL and the American 350SLC became a 450SLC. In Europe, the old 350SL and 350SLC continued in production alongside the 450SL and 450SLC models, which rapidly began to outsell them by a huge margin.

Clearly it had not been too difficult to remove the emissions-control gear from the M117 engine, and there is little doubt that certain illegal conversions had already been carried out in the USA by enthusiastic owners of the early 4½-litre cars! In European form, with a higher compression ratio and revised fuel and ignition settings, the 4½-litre V8 put out 225bhp, or 12½% more than its emissions-controlled brother. Torque was not much increased, but the extra power produced at lower crank-shaft speeds made the European 450 models more relaxing to drive than the 350s and American 4½-litres. Like their American equivalents, the European 4½-litres had anti-squat rear suspension to compensate for the huge torque available.

Like the SL, the SLC looks considerably more attractive when the optional alloy wheels are fitted, although these need constant cleaning to remove brake dust, especially at the front.

The side windows of the SLC are fully retractable, which can be a help when entering or leaving the rear compartment. Legroom is reasonable provided the front seats are not fully extended on their runners or their backrests inclined unduly.

Yet there was no time for Stuttgart to stand still: even though no major modifications were needed to meet the stricter 1974 regulations in America, late 1973 saw the motoring world shaken by the sudden realization that the days of cheap and plentiful petrol were over. War broke out in the Arab world, and it became clear that cars with horrifyingly inefficient engines like the emissions-controlled M117 would have to become things of the past in a future which could only bring a steady increase in oil prices.

1974: The 280SL and 280SLC

These thoughts must have induced some sort of panic among the Daimler-Benz engineers, but with characteristically Teutonic efficiency they thought their way through to a solution. Already available on the Mercedes-Benz parts shelf was the M110 twin-overhead-camshaft six-cylinder engine, which powered some of the larger saloons and the prestige variants of the medium-size saloons. With 185bhp in European form, it was some 15bhp down on even the smaller V8, but it certainly had enough power to satisfy many potential SL and SLC customers. Perhaps most significant of all, its 2.8 litres suggested it might be cheaper to run than 3½ or 4½ litres of V8; and at this time of widespread panic about fuel costs, launching cars with smaller engines looked like having good publicity value if nothing else. So from the autumn

The instrument and control layouts are similar for SL and SLC models, although each has undergone minor changes during the cars' long production runs.

of 1974, the existing W107s were supplemented in most markets (though not in Great Britain or the USA) by 280SL and 280SLC variants.

The 2,746cc M110 was in fact a relatively new engine, having seen the light of day in the W114 New Generation saloons and coupes in 1972. It was available in both carburetted and fuel-injected forms, the latter being the more powerful and being the choice for the W107s. Actually, the loss of 15bhp did not hurt the performance too much as compared to the 3½-litre models, as the six-cylinder engine was rather lighter and higher-revving. These higher engine speeds did make it slightly noisier than the V8s, though, and noise levels were not helped by the low 3.69:1 final drive, intended to keep acceleration figures respectable at the expense of top speed and fuel consumption. Perhaps to emphasize that the 280SL and 280SLC were the bottom models of the range rather than because of gearing considerations, the six-cylinder cars wore 185 × 14 rubber in place of the low-profile 70-section tyres of the V8s: customers who insisted, however, could have alloy wheels with 195/70 tyres (which were one size narrower than those specified on the V8s). One way or another, it seemed to make no difference to the cars' road behaviour.

The 2.8-litre engine brought with it two drive-trains new to the W107s, as well as a set of different ratios in its standard four-speed manual transmission. A rare option was the five-speed manual box with a 0.88:1 overdrive top, a variant of the box first seen in 1968; that brought with it an even lower final drive ratio of 3.92:1 to keep acceleration figures acceptable. More commonly specified was the new four-speed automatic with torque converter (Stuttgart had never *really* been convinced that three speeds were enough in an automatic transmission), which made the 280SL and 280SLC the only W107s ever to be available with this unit.

The policy of combining the radiator grille with the engine compartment cover means that both the grille and the radiator itself can be cleaned more readily, while headroom is only modestly impeded on SL and SLC models.

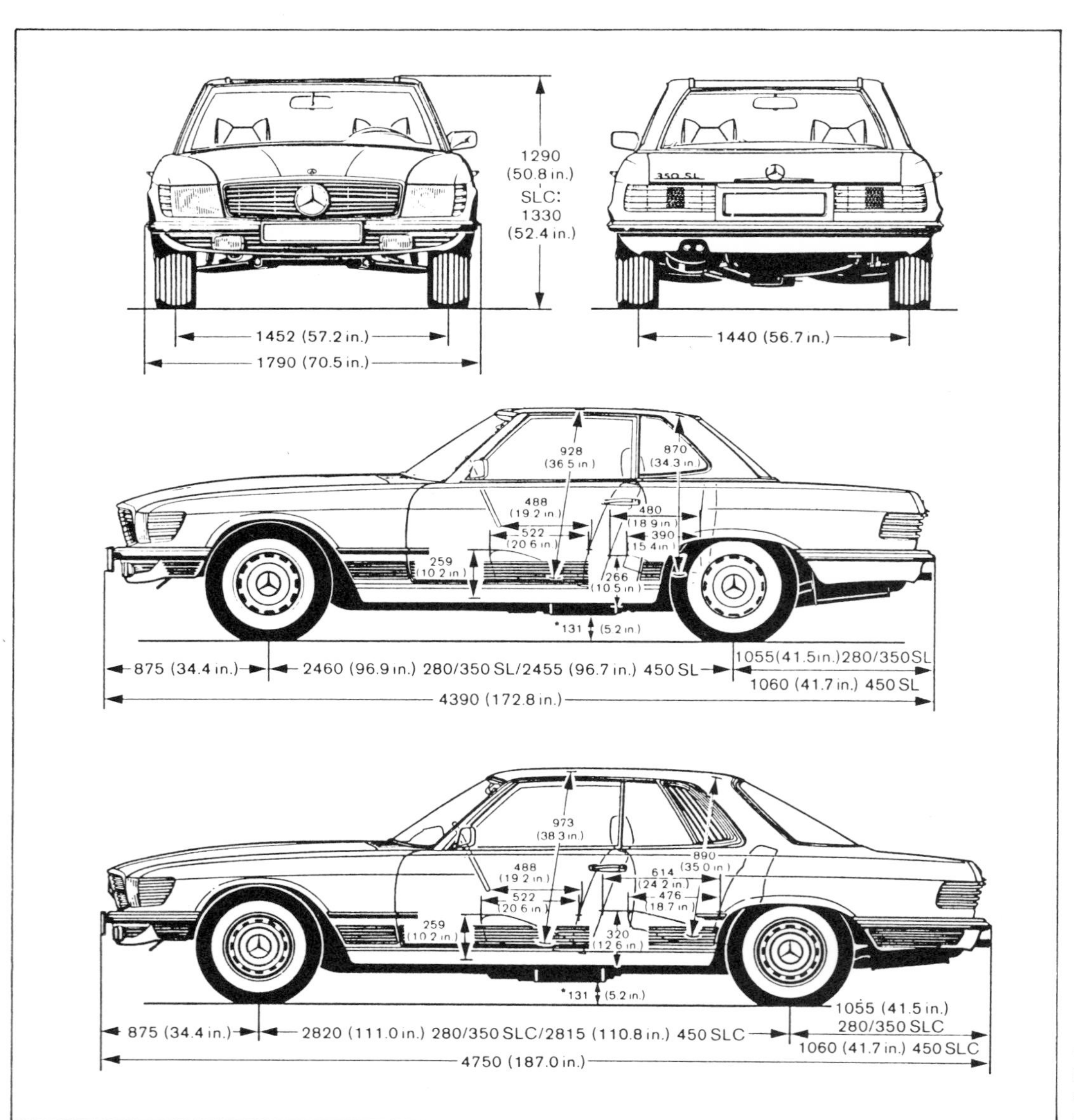

Drawings and dimensions which explain why the SL can only be considered as a two-seater for anything other than extreme emergencies whereas the SLC offers realistic 2 + 2 accommodation.

Originally fitted to cars earmarked for the US market, where they carried the designation 350SL (or SLC) 4.5, the 4.5-litre V8 engine became available in Europe from 1973. This is a British-market 450SL of that year, by which time head restraints had become a standard fitment.

The SL's optional steel hardtop is detachable as a unit complete with fixed side windows which, in conjunction with the wide rear screen, offer considerably better rearward vision than when the normal soft roof is erected.

The interior of a 450SL equipped with automatic transmission. The tweed-effect cloth upholstery was a popular choice during the late 1970s. Note that moving the clock from its original position in the centre of the facia to the lower part of the rev-counter dial has enabled five air intakes to be incorporated instead of the four fitted to early SLs.

A recent photograph of an immaculately maintained British-registered 450SL when not far short of its 10th birthday.

CHAPTER 3

California points the way

The 450SLC 5.0 begins a trend

For 1975, the smog-conscious State of California decided to go its own way with exhaust-emissions regulations, and introduced a set of rules even more stringent than those which applied in the rest of the USA. In order to conform, W107s sold in California had to be equipped with catalytic converters in the exhaust system. For 1975, Californian 4½-litre models were accordingly fitted with a converter on either side of their engines close up to the exhaust ports. Power was reduced to a quoted 180bhp by the SAE nett rating (or around the same figure by DIN standards), which, however, does not even hint at the full effect of the Californian modifications on the engine's behaviour. Owners complained that the M117 felt strangled and strained under certain conditions, and of course acceleration had suffered, too. Nevertheless, Daimler-Benz considered it worthwhile to go on producing this special variant in relatively limited numbers for California, because emissions-control legislation in the rest of the USA would catch up with California's in four years' time, and all North American cars would then need catalytic converters. The Californian models thus acted as a kind of customer clinic for the later North American cars.

By this stage, it was also beginning to look as though most of Europe would eventually follow the American lead in aiming for cleaner exhausts, and in anticipation of new regulations (which took over 10 years to come!) Stuttgart decided to fit Bosch K-Jetronic fuel injection to the V8 engines in place of the D-Jetronic system. The K-Jetronic was a mechanical system which lent itself more easily to the sort of tuning needed for emissions-control than the older electronic type, and had the additional advantages of being simpler and cheaper. It was fitted to the 4½-litre engines in November 1975 and to the 3½-litres from February 1976. In combination with other detail changes designed to promote cleaner exhausts, it brought the engines' power outputs down to 217bhp (from 225bhp) and 195bhp (from 200bhp) respectively; but in all fairness, performance was scarcely affected at all. Worries about the continuing availability of high-octane petrol caused Stuttgart to lower the compression ratio of the twin-cam 'six' at the same time as the new injection system was fitted, and this engine's power went down from 185bhp to 177bhp. Other 1976 changes included the arrival of a cruise control system operated from a convenient stalk on the steering column; but there were to be no more changes of significance until early 1978.

In the meantime, the 450SLC 5.0 stole upon the world. Although always intended as a limited-production model, it was a significant car for Daimler-Benz as it embodied the elements on which their future model strategy would be based – fuel-saving through the use of lightweight construction materials, together with yet bigger engines to offset the effects of exhaust-emissions controls. Pilot-production cars came off the lines in September 1977, and the 450SLC 5.0 made its bow at the Frankfurt Show later that autumn, although production cars would not become available until the following spring. Sales were initially restricted to the European market, while volume production of the new 5-litre engine built up from its original capacity limit of 80 units per month, and in fact the model was never available in the USA.

The 450SLC 5.0 was distinguished visually from the other SLC models by its dark-coloured lower body panels, and by a chin spoiler at the front and a discreet black spoiler across the

The extra chin spoiler and the dark lower body panels reveal that this is one of the special 450SLC 5.0 models.

rearmost edge of the boot-lid. The former feature was purely cosmetic, and was probably intended to prepare customers for the visual shock of the plastic lower panels which would arrive on 1979's W126 models; the spoilers, however, reduced aerodynamic drag by a claimed 9%. Of course, badging on the boot-lid helped to identify the car, too, and the 450SLC 5.0 was only available with the alloy wheels optional on other SLCs. No fewer than 125lb had also been trimmed from the car's weight, thanks to the use of lightweight aluminium, not only for the wheels but also for the bonnet and boot-lid panels. Steel boot-lids were nevertheless fitted to the few cars specially ordered without spoilers, which hinted that the spoiler had the additional function of bracing the lightweight panel. Yet the most remarkable weight-saving was found in the new 5-litre engine.

Based closely on the 4½-litre unit, with which it shared its 85mm stroke and M117 type-designation, the 5-litre engine saved no fewer than 95lb in weight through its light-alloy castings as against the cast-iron 4½-litre. The cylinder block, overbored from 92mm to 97mm to give a swept volume of 5,025cc, was cast from Reynolds 390 light alloy. This material, which had a silicon content of some 17%, had first been used by Chevrolet for the engine of their Vega, and was also seen in the engine of Porsche's new 928. As in the Vega, the bores were subjected after machining to a chemical etching process which removed a thin layer of aluminium, leaving the silicon particles standing slightly proud to form a wear-resistant surface. For additional strength, the block had external ribbing and extended well below the crankshaft centre-line. Not only the block, but also the heads, pistons, valve covers and sump, were all cast from light alloy, and even the iron casting of the K-Jetronic fuel injection unit had been changed for an alloy one.

In addition to saving weight, one of the major design aims of the 5-litre V8 had been to minimize its servicing requirements. Most notable was the replacement of the older engine's adjustable tappets by self-adjusting hydraulic tappets of the company's own design. Also of note were the special head gaskets (first seen on the 6.9-litre M100 engine) which eliminated the need for retorquing of the head bolts after a running-in period, and the

Badging of the car also helped to identify it, as did the small rear spoiler.

way in which all the auxiliary drives were grouped at the front of the engine, with a common duplex chain serving the single overhead camshaft on each cylinder bank, a single chain driving the oil pump, and four rubber V-belts serving water pump and alternator, viscous-coupled fan, power steering pump and air conditioning pump. The new engine's claimed power output was 240bhp DIN, 15bhp more than the European 4½-litre in its highest state of tune, and its increased torque of 297lb/ft allowed the fitting of an extremely high 2.72:1 axle ratio. Top speed of the 450SLC 5.0 with its standard three-speed automatic transmission was a genuine 140mph with a blistering 0-60mph time a full second faster than the 4½-litre car; but much more significant in terms of the way Mercedes-Benz engineering was going was that the fuel consumption of 16mpg was *also* better than that of the smaller-engined car. No manual gearbox was ever made available for the 450SLC 5.0, as Stuttgart had nothing on the shelf which could withstand the engine's massive torque and considered proprietary gearboxes to be too unrefined. Nevertheless, some enthusiastic owners had their cars fitted with Getrag or ZF five-speed boxes.

Throughout its production life, the 450SLC 5.0 remained

Spoilers at both ends and dark lower side panels are in evidence in this shot of the 450SLC 5.0.

The new light-alloy V8 engine which would power the big Mercedes-Benz cars of the 1980s was first seen in 5-litre form in the 450SLC 5.0. No other car would have it in exactly this form, as the bore diameter was reduced when the engine went into large-scale production.

something of a rarity, and fewer than 3,000 were built before production stopped in 1981. Yet it allowed Stuttgart to gain valuable experience of the new engine in service (one might suggest cynically that it was at the expense of some of their more well-heeled customers!), and this experience did lead to design changes before the new engine went into full-scale production.

The last years of the cast-iron V8s, 1977-1980

From the moment the new light-alloy V8 appeared, it was clear that the days of the cast-iron V8s must be numbered, especially as its appearance was accompanied by well-founded rumours that a 3.8-litre version was on the stocks to replace the 3½-litre M116. Nevertheless, the 3½-litre and 4½-litre models remained available until autumn 1980. Production of the 350SL actually stopped in March 1980, but the 450SL carried on until November the same year in order to satisfy the continuing North American demand. In the meantime, fears about engine damage resulting from the use of lower-octane fuels seemed to have been allayed, and compression ratios were raised again during 1978, the 2.8-litre engines going back up to 185bhp, but at the reduced engine speed of 5,800rpm, and the 3½-litres up to 205bhp; the 4½-litres went back up to 225bhp later that year. These power figures were for the European engines, of course. The North American cars suffered even more after the obligatory introduction in spring 1979 of three-way catalytic converters in their exhaust systems, which may have reduced noxious emissions, but did nothing for the power output, now down to 160bhp. Still, associated piston, camshaft and exhaust manifold changes were

The competition version of the 450SLC 5.0 which Björn Waldegaard drove in the 1979 Rally of Portugal.

accompanied by a new and higher final drive to give better fuel economy in the sort of driving most common in North America's 55mph blanket speed limit – and Stuttgart no longer had to produce a special Californian version of the car, either.

The last years of the cast-iron V8s also witnessed some minor changes to the cars' interiors. Thus, in the spring of 1977, a fifth air vent on the dashboard replaced the centrally-mounted clock, which was henceforth incorporated within one of the main dials. At the end of 1979, an Econometer was added, which showed the driver how irresponsibly he was squandering his petrol if he ever bothered to look at it, and the detachable glove box lamp was replaced by a fixed unit. Then the console was tidied up in the early months of the following year.

Of the four engine sizes available in the W107 models between 1971 and 1980, it was hardly surprising to find that the 4½-litre had been the most popular, and by a huge margin. Sales, of course, had been considerably boosted by the fact that for some years it was the only engine available in W107s sold in the USA. Next most popular was the 3½-litre V8, although its sales had dropped off sharply after the arrival of the 2.8-litre models. Bringing up the rear in almost penny numbers was the 5-litre V8, which engine would nevertheless be at the forefront of the W107 model line-up for the 1980s.

1981: The 380SL, 380SLC, 500SL and 500SLC

From the autumn of 1980, the 3½-litre and 4½-litre models were directly replaced by essentially similar cars powered by a pair of new, fuel-efficient, light-alloy V8s. The 350SL and SLC ceded to 380SL and SLC models of similar performance, while the 450SL and SLC cars were replaced by much quicker 500SL and 500SLC variants. The 450SLC 5.0 carried on for an extra year, overlapping with the more expensive new 5-litre models, and the 280SL and SLC continued as before. Visual distinctions were limited to badging, except in the case of the new 5-litre models,

The badging has changed, and the twin-barrelled exhaust now points downward, but otherwise the rear of this 380SL is distinguished from that of earlier models only by its badging.

which wore as standard the alloy wheels optional on other models and had the same spoilers as the 450SLC 5.0. On SL models, both hard and soft tops were now standard equipment.

Although the 5-litre engine was still claimed to put out 240bhp, its swept volume had actually been slightly reduced from the 5,025cc of the original production engine to 4,973cc, thanks to narrower cylinder bores. The reduction in bore size of 0.5mm allowed more 'meat' between the bores and consequently permitted water passages where there had hitherto been none. The new 'small' V8 brought no real surprises, having essentially the same relationship to the old 3½-litre as the new 5-litre had to the old 4½-litre. With a displacement of 3,818cc thanks to a stroke increased from 65.8mm to 71.8mm, it boasted 218bhp and 224lb/ft of torque – both figures just up on those for the superseded engine. Most significant, as with the 5-litre unit, were the savings in weight consequent upon the light-alloy construction, and an improvement in fuel consumption.

American-market engines were quite radically different from their European counterparts in the case of the smaller V8, however. In order to keep within the emissions-control rules and achieve a satisfactory performance, Daimler-Benz engineers had to alter the shape of the combustion chambers by changing the ratio of bore to stroke. The bore was thus reduced from 92mm to 88mm while the stroke went up from 71.8mm to 78.9mm; swept volume went up from 3,818cc to 3,839cc. American-market models, as usual, were rather slower than the European versions, but the European 380SL would run to 127mph, while 139mph and 0-60mph in 7.8 seconds were claimed for the 5-litre car. Road test figures actually improved on these, making a 500SL marginally faster than the (albeit much heavier) 450SEL 6.9. Both SLs and SLCs remained beautifully-balanced machines in the best Mercedes-Benz tradition, despite the changed weight distribution caused by the lighter engines, but both were rather tail-happy by the standards of the 1980s, and the 500SL in particular could exhibit some interesting rear-end behaviour if all the engine's torque was put through the rear wheels at once. Fortunately, few people drove such expensive cars with the sort of abandon necessary to provoke these on-the-limit failings.

The only transmission available in the 3.8-litre and 5-litre W107s was a new and lightweight version of the four-speed automatic first seen in the 2.8-litre models. The torque converter which went with this was of smaller diameter than earlier types to reduce mechanical losses in the transmission, and thus operated more quickly and efficiently over a wider speed range. It contributed both to increased driving pleasure and decreased fuel consumption. All the V8 cars had a limited-slip differential, and the 5-litre models inherited the extremely high 2.72:1 axle ratio of the lightweight 450SLC 5.0, while the 3.8-litre variants had rather lower 3.27:1 gearing. Even so, there was enough engine torque available at tickover speeds to make for undesirable 'creep', and so the new automatic gearboxes were programmed to change up to second gear at idle, and back to first only when the accelerator was depressed. Overall weights were improved not only by the new light-alloy engines, but also by the standardization of the aluminium alloy body panels first seen on the 450SLC 5.0. Fuel economy was thus marginally better than on the superseded models, without loss of performance.

The ABS anti-lock braking system was introduced as an option on all the W107 models in autumn 1980, but there were no further changes of note until the following autumn, when the W107s were subjected to the 'Energy Concept' fuel-saving revisions which affected all other current production models as well. Axle ratios were raised on all the SLs and SLCs, and the new Sindelfingen-built GL275 five-speed manual gearbox with its overdrive fifth gear was standardized on the 2.8-litre models. When the optional automatic transmission was fitted to these cars, it was henceforward the same as that which was standard on the bigger-engined W107s. The 5-litre V8 had a higher compression ratio and revised valve timing, losing 5bhp in the process, but developing its maximum output at a slightly lower crankshaft speed; but the biggest change of all was to the European M116 3.8-litre engine, which adopted the bore and stroke dimensions of its American-market counterpart. Production of the 3,818cc version stopped altogether. The 'new' European engine had a

This is one of the smaller-engined second-generation W107 roadsters, with the additional chin spoiler but no bootlid spoiler.

The 500SL, showing its bootlid spoiler. The Germans gave this piece of aerodynamic addenda the uncomplimentary name of 'rubber sausage'!

raised compression ratio and revised valve timing just like its larger brother, and similarly lost 14bhp, although maximum power was now available at a lower crankshaft speed.

Although the 380SL went on to be the most popular of the later SL variants, very few 380SLC models were built for Europe with the revised engine, for the SLC in all its variants ceased production in autumn 1981: only those cars built between spring and the end of production had the European 3,839cc engine. The SLC's replacement, of course, was not related to the two-seaters but, as in the days before the W107 when the prestige coupes and cabriolets had been saloon-based, was a development of the luxurious S-class saloon.

1985: The 300SL and 420SL

The 1985 Frankfurt Show saw the introduction of what must surely be the final variants of the W107 SLs, which were scheduled for replacement in 1987 by the new R129 roadster models. The 500SL continued in production, but the 280SL and 380SL were directly replaced by new models bearing the designations 300SL and 420SL.

All three 1986-season W107s came with a redesigned chin spoiler, which was claimed to reduce front end lift by 30%. The short production life foreseen for these models had deterred Stuttgart from making the modifications which would allow the new traction aids introduced at Frankfurt to be fitted, but the

The complete second-generation W107 SL range, in all three body guises. A 280SL wears the hardtop, a 380SL demonstrates the soft top in position, and a 500SL is shown in open form.

Showing the US-specification bumpers and lights, this is a 380SL for that market. The W107s have been hugely popular in North America, for which they had primarily been designed.

1986-season models did have revised front wheel geometry, plus bigger and more powerful disc brakes made feasible by the use of lower-profile (65%.aspect ratio) tyres on 15-inch alloy wheels of the new flush-faced design seen elsewhere in the Mercedes-Benz range. Inside the cars were better contoured seats and a new and more comprehensive instrument panel, while outside there were new flush-fitting door handles.

The engine for the 300SL was the larger of two new straight-

Front and rear compartments of a cloth-upholstered 380SL with the optional rear seat. Children can be carried in the back in tolerable comfort if the front seats are brought well forward.

A leather-trimmed 500SL. In this instance colour contrasting is confined to the facia and centre console.

six power units first seen in the new medium-size W124 saloons on their announcement in 1984, while the 4.2-litre engine of the 420SL was the latest big-bore version of the M116 V8, which was also to be seen in the S-class 420SE, SEL and SEC models similarly launched at Frankfurt in 1985.

The new 3-litre six-cylinder engine and its 2.6-litre partner (first seen installed in the 260E saloon) shared the same 80.2mm stroke and allegedly their basic design was related to a four-cylinder 1.6-litre engine which had been developed for the W201 compact saloon range but not put into production. Instead of the twin overhead camshafts found in the superseded M110 engine, which now remained in production only for the off-road G-Wagen, the new M103s both reverted to a single-overhead-camshaft layout in the interests of reducing internal friction, and in line with recent practice they were equipped with the Bosch KE-Jetronic electro-mechanical fuel injection, which lent itself most readily to fine-tuning for efficient control of exhaust emissions. They had only four main bearings, where previously seven would have been the norm, but they were wonderfully smooth and free-revving units in which the extra three bearings

By normal sports car standards the SL's luggage accommodation is generous, and of course the rear trunk can be augmented by making use of the rear seat area when only two people are being carried.

were not missed. Construction, as dictated by contemporary Stuttgart practice, relied extensively on the use of lightweight alloys, and features like the cooling fan with both viscous and thermostatic couplings were only to be expected by this stage.

Apart from its larger cylinder bores, the 420SL's engine differed from the superseded M116 all-alloy 3.8-litre V8 in having modified combustion chambers, larger inlet and exhaust valves, together with the new CIS-E fuel injection and, without exhaust catalysers, it enjoyed a 14bhp advantage over its predecessor. A similar improvement in power was also offered by minor changes to the 5-litre V8, which included improved breathing through a modified intake system with larger inlet valves, free-flow exhaust manifolds, a new electronic ignition system and the CIS-E fuel injection system.

From autumn 1985, Stuttgart began to offer cars equipped with the MF-system and catalytic converters to suit both American and forthcoming European emissions-control legislation, beginning with various fuel-injected engines. Although there were no plans to offer the 500SL with the MF fuel and ignition adapter system (a variant with catalytic converters in the exhaust system was, of course, already made for the US market), both the new SL models were destined to have it, the 300SL from early 1986 and the 420SL by October that year. Inevitably, the effect of the emissions-control equipment was to stifle some of the performance otherwise available, but it was a tribute to the development work which had been going on at Stuttgart for nearly 20 years that the power losses were now minimal – around 10bhp for the six-cylinder engine. A comparison with the

The two-tone door trim of a cloth-upholstered 380SL.

massive power losses suffered by the detoxed Federal engines of the mid-1970s reveals just how far Stuttgart had advanced, but the fact that it had taken over a decade to reach the stage where detoxed and non-detoxed engines' power outputs were broadly comparable is a reminder of just how difficult it has been for automobile engineers to match engine design to legislative requirements.

For those who chose to buy their 300SL in its optimum performance mode, as introduced in autumn 1985, the 2,962cc 'six' offered a healthy 187bhp with abundant torque, giving the car a maximum speed of 127mph, or as much as the superseded 380SL, while the 218bhp of the 4,196cc V8 engine conferred a 133mph top speed on the 420SL version of the W107. The 500SL thus remained the quickest variant, and it was interesting that the new 5.6-litre V8 seen at the 1985 Frankfurt Show in the latest S-class saloons and coupes was not put into the SLs. No doubt the W107's rear suspension, already near its limit with the 5-litre engine, simply could not handle the extra torque.

The SL's future

By autumn 1985, when these words were being penned, the basic W107 SL shape had been in production for 15 years – far longer than any previous two-seater from Stuttgart. For a design so long in the tooth, however, it had worn very well indeed, and sales were certainly showing no signs of falling off. To some extent, the popularity of aftermarket styling kits had helped to rejuvenate the body style for those who were not entirely happy with it, but it must be said that most of these kits tended to make the SL look heavier and clumsier rather than improving its appearance.

A new SL model, coded R129 and by all accounts closely

An immaculate 1983 500SL in white with contrasting grey hardtop, which had covered less than 3,000 miles when it was sold by Greenoaks Garages Ltd of South Croydon, Surrey, early in 1986.

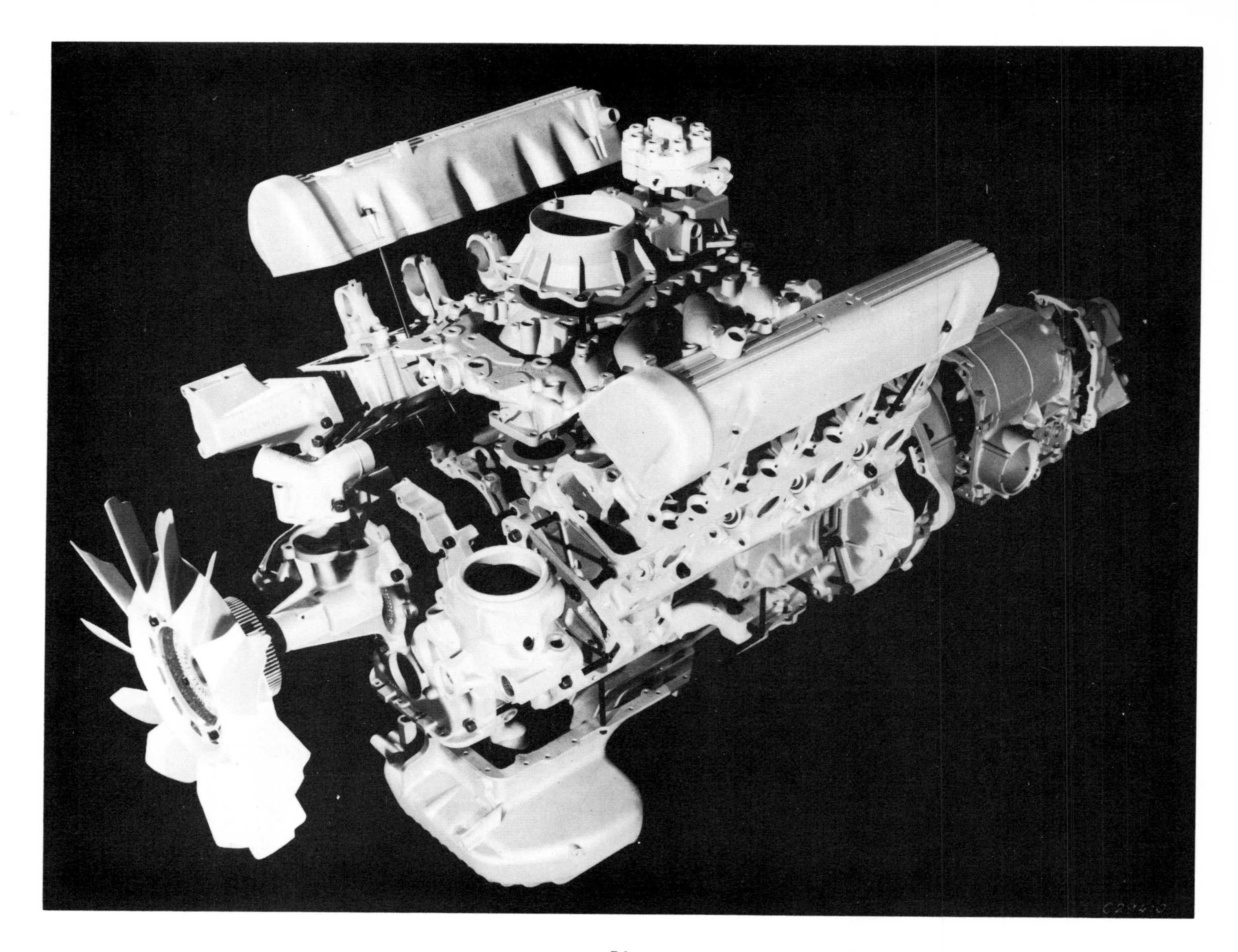

The historically famous 300SL name returned to the Mercedes-Benz catalogue in 1985 with the introduction of a new 3-litre single-OHC six-cylinder engine in place of the twin-OHC 2.8-litre 'six'. Clear identification features of this final development of the long-running W107 SL line are the wider spoiler and the distinctive new wheels.

Left, a cleverly contrived picture illustrating the major components of the light-alloy V8 engines developed for use in SL models and S-class saloons in the early 1980s. The crankcase is a low-pressure die-casting in an aluminium alloy containing silicon, and the cylinder surfaces are chemically treated to expose a thin layer of silicon crystals which provide a low-wearing surface for the chromium-plated light-alloy pistons.

The new 3-litre engine, which develops 188bhp DIN at 5,700rpm, nestling neatly in the front compartment of the 300SL.

related in many of its styling details to the W201 compact saloons, was certainly on the stocks, but not expected in the showrooms before mid-1987 at the earliest. It seemed that the familiar SL pattern of an open car with both soft and hard tops would be followed, but that the R129 might have a true 2 + 2 seating configuration. There would be no experimentation with mid-mounted engines, though: the R129 was to use the traditional Mercedes-Benz front-engine/rear-wheel-drive layout, with the engine mounted conventionally north/south. When it finally does arrive, the W107s will remain eagerly-sought-after cars, just like the W113 roadsters before them, for their classic status is already assured.

The 500SL can be differentiated from the 420SL alongside it by its rear spoiler. These two cars demonstrate the choice of either cloth or leather upholstery in the SL range.

300SL hardtop–a splendid autobahn cruiser.

The 300SL in hardtop form is a car of classic appearance, destined to remain one of the most covetable of cars long after the W107 series ceases production.

CHAPTER 4

Safety with style

The W116 S-class cars

The S-class W116 range probably did more for the image of Daimler-Benz as a quality car manufacturer than any other model. It combined an advanced technical specification with the refinement expected of a top-notch luxury saloon in a more balanced fashion than any previous Mercedes-Benz, and throughout its production run was widely regarded to be the best saloon car available anywhere in the world. Evidence of the high regard in which it was held is to be found in the sales figures: a total of 473,035 W116s were built in seven seasons of production, or 100,000 more than the total of W108/109 S-class cars which the W116 superseded. These figures are all the more remarkable when seen against the background of a gradually strengthening Deutschmark, which made the S-class very expensive to buy and maintain outside West Germany; and against the effects of the oil crisis and the consequent rise in fuel costs which turned buyers very much against thirsty, big-engined cars.

Development of the W116 began in 1966, one year after the introduction of the range it was to replace and six years before it would itself reach the showrooms. Such a long lead-time illustrates how much care went into the design, but the fact that even the body sheet-metal was not finally settled until 1969 tends to suggest that the arrival of the superb Jaguar XJ6 in 1968 held up the W116's development a little until Stuttgart's engineers had got the measure of this new rival. It was to be three more years before engineering chief Hans Scherenberg was satisfied that the W116 had achieved all its original design aims, as well as those new ones imposed by the XJ6's excellence, and that it was ready to be released.

Probably the most significant aim was that of meeting the Federal regulations without sacrificing any of the qualities associated with Mercedes-Benz. In terms of the bodyshell, this implied increases in both size and weight, and the extra 5 inches in the W116's wheelbase over that of its predecessor was all used up in the interests of structural safety, for there was no extra length in the passenger cabin. Some sacrifice had to be made in the boot space as well, and there was a cubic foot less of luggage-room in the W116 thanks to a decision to limit the overall length increase to 2 inches, despite the longer wheelbase. The W116 was also 2 inches wider than the W108/109 cars, but because of improved side-impact protection in the doors it actually offered *less* interior width.

In the late 1960s, Daimler-Benz was one of the very few European car manufacturers to have its own wind-tunnel, and the resultant awareness of aerodynamics at Stuttgart had its effect on the W116 shape. Like the W107 sports models, the body had a very slight wedge-shape, with a bonnet-line much lower than that of its predecessors. Some thought was given to streamlining the front end even more by using the 'sports' air intake of the SL models, and indeed the W116-based ESF 22 research vehicle of 1973 had such a design, but the proposal was abandoned before production began. Nevertheless, aerodynamic considerations kept the height of the traditional saloon grille down, and to compensate for the attendant reduction in cooling area, a huge radiator air intake was sited below the front bumper. For the first time, the three-pointed star mascot was mounted on a pivot atop the grille – but despite what photographs of the cars at speed may suggest, this was to minimize the danger to pedestrians rather than contribute to the streamlining!

By the early 1970s, Stuttgart was making use of sophisticated computer technology. Here a ⅕ scale model of the W116 is 'scanned' three-dimensionally. The information stored on punched tape could then be used to guide a machine which would automatically draw the car or parts of it to any desired scale.

The windscreen was much more steeply raked than before, again to cut down drag as well as wind-noise at speed, when specially-shaped rain-deflectors on the screen pillars would also help to keep the side windows clear of water and road dirt. The ribbed lenses first seen on the W107s helped the front indicators and rear lamps to remain visible in poor conditions, and even the door mirrors were designed to be as aerodynamically efficient as possible. The W116 actually *looked* more streamlined than its predecessors, too, thanks to an actual reduction of an inch in overall height and an apparent reduction in height brought about by the low-mounted belt-line rubbing-strip. From the front and rear, the vertical light clusters also contributed to the low line; but none of this attention lavished on streamlining, both real and apparent, could altogether compensate for the fact that the W116 was a large car with a big frontal area, and that it was very much heavier than its predecessors.

This weight increase amounted to about 9% over the previous S-class cars in European trim, and was almost entirely due to structural requirements arising out of the Federal safety regulations. Obviously, Stuttgart wanted to avoid the cost of having very different European and North American W116s in production, and so the bodyshell design was common to both. Based on the Mercedes-patent 'safety cell' used in all the company's new models since 1959, with its progressively

The ⅕ scale model and the full-scale wooden mock-up of the W116. It is noteworthy that the full-scale model has twin circular headlamps, apparently behind a single rectangular glass panel. On production cars, the wipers parked on the opposite side of the screen.

collapsible front and rear crumple zones, the W116 nevertheless had a more rigid central cell than ever, with much greater roll-over stiffness and side-impact resistance than its predecessors. The crumple zones were also weaker, that at the front having forked side-members to help control distortion caused by a head-on collision. There were other new features, too. Previous Mercedes-Benz practice had been to stow the spare wheel upright in the boot, but one lesson learned from the series of ESF vehicles in the late 1960s and early 1970s was to position the spare below the boot floor, where it acted as a buffer in the case of a rear-end shunt. The fuel tank, also with the effects of a rear-end shunt in view, was sited as far as possible from the rear bumper over the back axle, and it had a special filler neck which would crush rather than shear off in an accident. Running in parallel

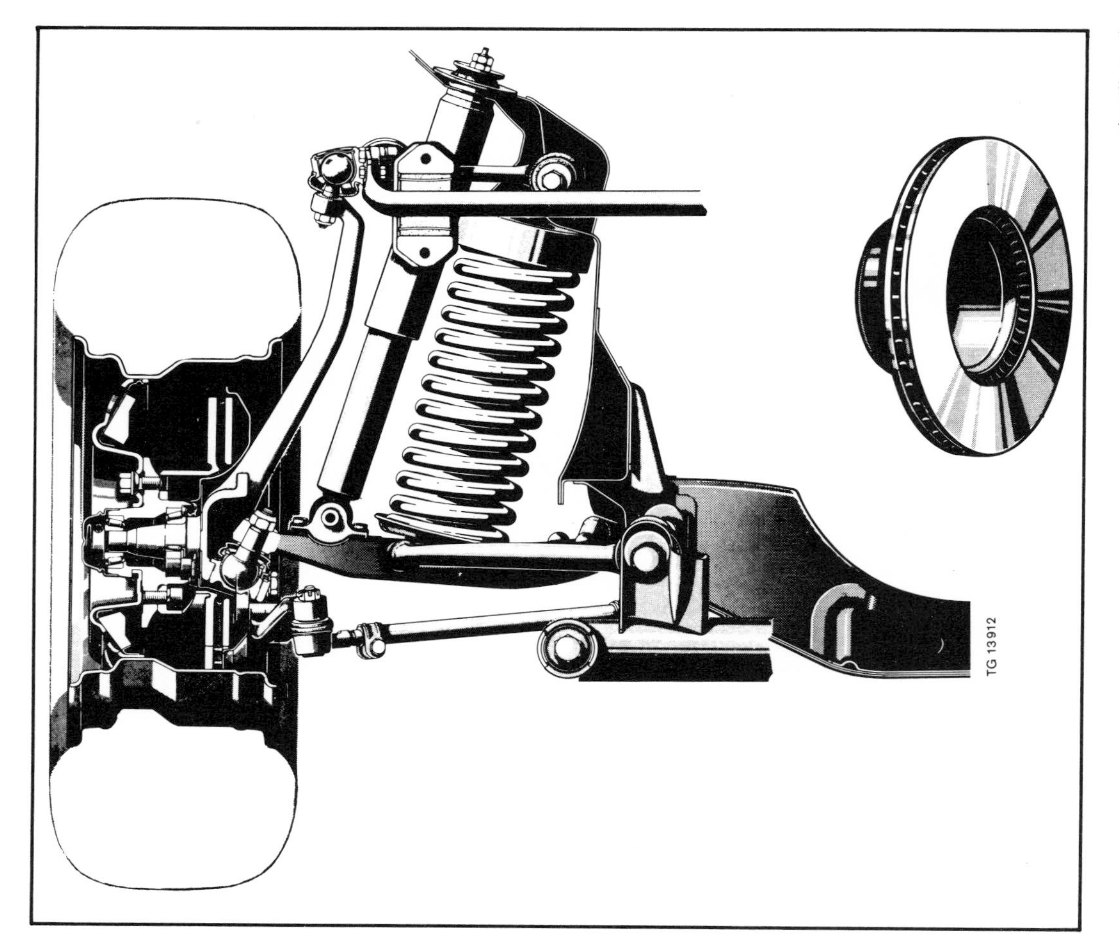

The W116 front suspension was a revision of the coil-and-wishbone layout seen on earlier Mercedes-Benz models. Inset, right, is the ventilated disc of the front brakes.

with the programme to achieve structural safety, Scherenberg had organized a weight-saving programme under which every component was analysed in detail to ensure that it was of minimum weight for the strength required. Without this programme, the W116 weight penalty would surely have been greater than that 9%; as it was, Federal requirements eventually dictated that the North American cars would be heavier still.

One area in which weight had been saved almost accidentally was that of the front suspension. The front wheels of earlier Mercedes-Benz cars had been mounted on a detachable subframe which traced its ancestry back to 1953's Ponton models, but the need to allow extra space under the W116's bonnet for the wide V8 engines with their various ancillaries had led to a redesign of the familiar wishbone-and-coil-spring layout in which the front

Cutaway drawing of a 350SE in its production form. The W116 design was packed with safety features, including extensive padding of the interior structure and equipment, a collapsible telescopic steering column and massive front and rear impact protection.

pivots of the lower wishbones were bolted directly to the bodyshell. Their rear pivots were attached to a light detachable cross-tube. There were simple transverse upper links, and the wheels were located fore-and-aft by short cranks reaching back from these upper links to an anti-roll bar mounted to the bulkhead at two points. Telescopic dampers were positioned outboard of the coil springs, inclined slightly inwards. The suspension geometry was carefully arranged to give anti-dive characteristics, and the new layout meant that the suspension loads were fed into a very rigid part of the body structure. An additional benefit was that the front-end sheet metal was left free to absorb crash energy without interference from the suspension links.

This reworked suspension had actually been developed from that of the Wankel-engined C-111 research vehicles, and its zero-offset steering geometry was a very advanced feature for the time. In the usual positive-offset geometry, the axis about which the front wheels pivot intersects the ground inboard of the tyre's contact patch, and this minimizes the effort needed at the steering wheel while sacrificing a certain amount of feel and stability. The Daimler-Benz engineers reasoned that power-assistance for the steering removed the problem of increased steering effort created by putting the steering axis at the centre of the tyre contact patch, and allowed the better feel and stability associated with zero-offset steering to be regained. Even better, the zero-offset layout permitted a tighter steering lock, and the turning circle of the W116 cars was 10 inches smaller than that of their shorter and narrower predecessors. All models had the same suspension set-up, and so had power-assisted steering, which, as usual, was of recirculating-ball type.

Just as a car tends to nose-dive under heavy braking when weight is transferred forwards, so the same weight-transfer

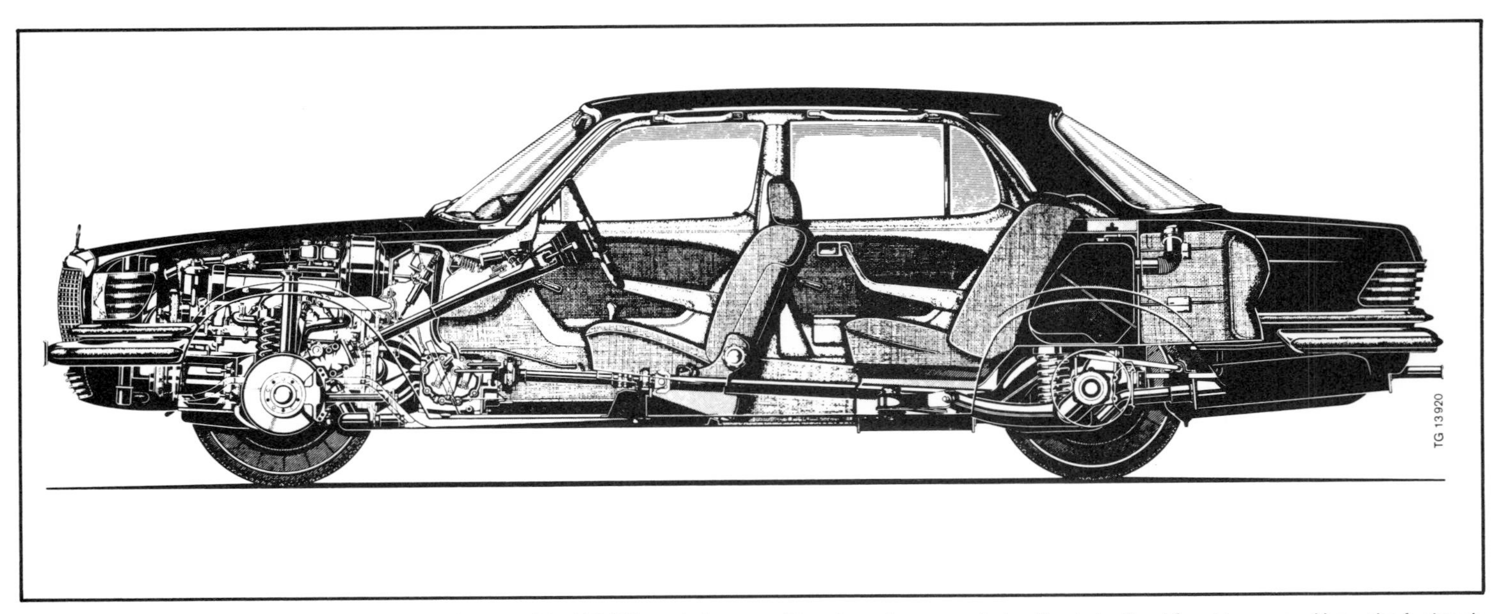

This longitudinal section of a 350SE shows the layout of the W116's main features. Note how the transmission line is inclined front to rear and how the fuel tank fits neatly above the rear axle and forward of the capacious luggage compartment.

phenomenon tends to cause rear-end squat under hard acceleration. In the W116 rear suspension, the geometry was arranged to eliminate this characteristic. Basically, the system was of the semi-trailing arm variety as seen in the New Generation Mercedes-Benz saloons introduced in the autumn of 1967. In order to insulate the body from axle and road noise, the trailing arms pivoted from a V-shaped fabricated steel subframe, itself attached to the body by three large-diameter rubber bushes. The noise-insulation properties of this system were impressive, but not, to Stuttgart's chagrin, as great as those of the Jaguar XJ6 rear suspension. Telescopic shock absorbers were concentric with the nearly vertical coil springs mounted in the centre of the trailing arms, and a cranked anti-roll bar mounted above the wheel centre-line completed the picture.

There was never any doubt that the W116 would be a fast car – indeed, a very fast car in one of its later derivatives – and so an all-disc braking system was specified, with ventilated discs on the front wheels and solid discs at the rear. As usual, the hydraulic system was split for safety, and there was vacuum servo-assistance. Brakes, however, were something which Stuttgart had got basically right several years earlier. It was not so with interior styling; which had been one of the weakest suits of the 1960s models; and here, a special effort was made for the W116.

Paramount among the interior design aims, as usual, had been crash-safety, and the first impression given to those entering the car was of massive strength and solidity. Crash padding was to be seen on almost every surface, and a neat lidded cubby-hole in the rear parcels shelf contained a comprehensive first-aid kit. Inertia-reel seat belts were standard for the front occupants, and were neatly concealed when not in use behind the B-pillar trim, emerging when required through slots. Rear seat belts, with their inertia-reels concealed beneath the rear parcels shelf, could also be fitted.

One of the strangest features of the interior was to be seen on

The neat and functional dashboard of the S-class models borrowed much from the W107 sports cars of 1971. This example has the relatively uncommon four-speed manual gearbox.

In this shot of a French-registered W116, the rain deflectors on the windscreen pillars and the shaped tops to the door trims, which act as wind-deflectors when the windows are open, are clearly visible. This car has the optional electric steel sunroof.

The wedge-shape of the body can be seen in this picture of a later vehicle fitted with the optional headlamp wash/wipe system and rear headrests to match those at the front. Note the massive wiper arms, which are somewhat untidy when not in use, but nevertheless very effective.

the door trims, which curved gracefully up towards the rear of each door and formed a wedge-shape above the lower edge of the window. Their purpose was inspired by the Daimler-Benz wind-tunnel: they deflected the air stream along the sides of the car when the windows were open! Like much of the rest of the interior, these trims were made of injection-moulded plastic, which in conjunction with the standard MB-Tex seats with cloth inserts was not everyone's idea of a luxury car's interior; but leather or velour seats could be had at a price, and anyway the character of the W116's interior lay in its satisfyingly functional and well-integrated design.

Behind the large four-spoke 'safety' steering-wheel were three

Despite its bulk, the S-class was a sleek design for its time, as this photograph demonstrates so clearly. The thickness of the door and screen pillars, however, was a subject of some criticism.

dials in a pleasantly-curved nacelle which recalled the W107 SL layout. Heater, radio and other auxiliary controls were relegated to a central console, and the gear-lever on both manual and automatic-transmission versions was sited on the transmission tunnel. As usual, a single stalk control on the steering-column operated lights, washers and wipers. Left-hand-drive cars all had the foot-operated parking brake which suited American tastes, but on right-hand-drive models there was an umbrella-type handbrake outboard of the steering-wheel. The seats were large and firm, and those at the front had fore-and-aft adjustment as well as variable backrest rake, squab height and angle. Rear legroom was not especially good for a large luxury car, but the low waistline, high seats and large glass area all made the interior seem lighter and roomier than it was. Heating and ventilation had the usual independent controls for driver and passenger, plus ducting into all four doors along the lines of the system first seen in the W107 sports models.

Stuttgart was at pains in some of its sales literature to point out that the new and sophisticated features which characterized the W116 models were not just there as a gimmick, but were part of an overall concept. At the heart of the W116 had lain the philosophy of 'co-ordinated integration'. What this meant, in the company's own words, was that 'the performance, safety, comfort and driving characteristics of the Mercedes-Benz S-class cars come together as one total entity in which all these features are matched one with another. They create the ability to cope with traffic and environmental problems and so relieve the driver of some of the stress by utilizing design-features that take fully

All W116 models for the American market had twin round headlamps to meet local regulations. For 1974, they also had massive bumpers on hydraulic shock-absorbing rams which as these pictures demonstrate, did nothing for the lines of the car.

The W116 was launched in Great Britain just before Easter 1973, and here one of the first vehicles to cross the Channel is being put through its paces. On RHD cars, the wipers parked on the other side of the screen, so as not to impede forward vision.

into account man's psychological and physical capabilities'. Copy-writer's gush, no doubt, and none the better for being translated rather too literally from the German – but it did sum up why the W116 models felt so beautifully balanced, as if everything formed part of a harmonious whole.

1972: The 280S, 280SE and 350SE

The first three models of the new S-class were introduced at the Paris Motor Show in September 1972, and the W108/109 models disappeared from the range. The new 280S and 280SE models directly replaced the old cars of the same name, while the new 350SE replaced the 280SE 3.5. For the time being, none of the new models was available in North America, where the old S-class cars continued to be available in showrooms until dealer stocks ran out; and there were no new long-wheelbase cars to replace the SEL variants of the old S-class.

The engines were all familiar from the old S-class cars, the two six-cylinder models running the M110 twin-overhead-camshaft engine of 2,746cc in carburetted (280S) or fuel-injected (280SE) form, while the M116 fuel-injected 3,499cc V8 went into the 350SE. There were performance differences, to be sure, but these were scarcely significant below about 70mph. In truth, it was equipment levels which principally distinguished the new cars. The 350SE, for example, had the best roadholding of the three models thanks to its new low-profile radial tyres; the two six-cylinder cars had conventional rubber. The 350SE could only be had with the W3A 040 three-speed automatic transmission, but the 280S and 280SE both came with a four-speed synchromesh box as standard and a four-speed automatic option. Not all markets were treated to the full range: for example, the 280S was considered by the UK importers to be too sparsely-equipped for the image which Mercedes-Benz enjoyed, so imports were stopped after only a few cars had been sold.

Initial test reports of the W116 were very enthusiastic about

An extra 4 inches in the wheelbase and consequently longer rear doors, plus different badging on the boot-lid, were all that distinguished the long-wheelbase models visually from the standard cars. This is an early 450SEL.

Nevertheless, the increase in rear legroom was appreciable. This is the spacious interior of a 450SEL. Note the impression of strength and solidity about the interior design.

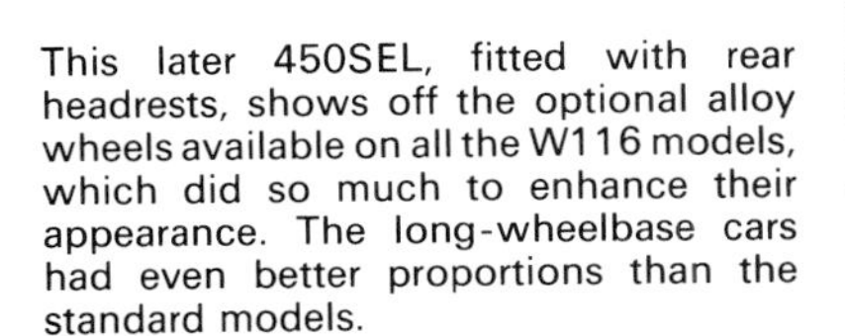

This later 450SEL, fitted with rear headrests, shows off the optional alloy wheels available on all the W116 models, which did so much to enhance their appearance. The long-wheelbase cars had even better proportions than the standard models.

Daimler-Benz publicity liked to stress the family resemblance among the various ranges, and this picture of a trio of British-registered cars was designed to make exactly that point. From left to right, a 280SE, a W107 450SL and a 450SEL, all dating from mid-1973.

everything except road noise, acceleration and maximum speeds. The great weight of the bodyshell meant that even a 350SE was 2-3mph down on the top speed of the old 280SE 3.5, and its 0-60mph acceleration times were very much poorer. Nevertheless, the 350SE was praised for its ability to sustain 120mph cruising – very close to its maximum speed – without strain on man or machinery, and its handling was highly rated as inspiring confidence. Comfort, build quality, the foolproof controls and the wealth of safety features all gained favourable comment, and the reassuring feeling given to braking by the anti-drive, anti-squat suspension was described as far in advance of any other production car. Yet there was even better to come.

1973: The 450SE and 450SEL

Although pilot-production of W116 models with the 4½-litre V8 engine had occurred at the same time as that of the smaller-engined versions, full production was slow to get under way and did not begin before December 1972. As a result, Daimler-Benz held over the launch of the cars until the Geneva Show in spring 1973, when the 4½-litre W116 cars were released at the same time as the 4½-litre W107 cars for the European market.

Like its 3½-litre relative, the 4½-litre engine was only available with a three-speed torque converter transmission, though in this installation it was uprated to cope with the engine's extra torque and was known as the W3B 050. The 4½-litre power unit was, of course, a long-stroke engine with a very flat torque curve, putting out 217lb/ft as low as 1,000rpm, which was more than the maximum torque available from the 3½-litre unit at four times that engine speed! Despite its great weight, the 450SE would therefore turn in very impressive figures, with a top speed of 134mph and a 0-60mph time of just over 9 seconds if the upchanges were held manually. Maximum speed, then, was not far short of the still-unreplaced 300SEL 6.3's, although acceleration was not in the same league, partly because of the W116's extra weight, and partly because it was geared for relaxed and relatively economical high-speed cruising. Nonetheless, the wide

A comparison of the 2.8-litre six-cylinder twin-OHC engine and the 3.5-litre V8 single-OHC power unit with which the W116 range was introduced in 1973. The 'six' was available with either a dual compound carburettor or fuel injection, the V8 with injection only.

spread of torque meant that the car was capable of effortless overtaking in high-speed traffic, which was far more important than standing-start acceleration in terms of safety and driver-satisfaction.

If the 450SE did have its faults as a high-speed luxury saloon, one of them must have been the same disappointing rear legroom as had been noted in the smaller-engined models which used the same bodyshell. Throughout the 1960s, Daimler-Benz policy had been to offer a long-wheelbase version of their top saloons, and for the 1970s there was to be no change. Seen for the first time at Geneva alongside the 450SE was the new long-wheelbase S-class model.

Available initially only with the 4½-litre engine, the long-wheelbase W116 offered an extra 4 inches in the wheelbase, all of which went into the rear seating area. Upholstery was either leather or velours according to customer preference, and in some markets (but not in Great Britain), it was possible to order an electric division. There was a weight penalty, of course, but the 4½-litre V8 had so much power and torque in reserve that performance was barely affected; and, if anything, the extra length of the rear doors actually enhanced the already elegant styling. Motoring journalists were certainly in no doubt about the qualities of the new big Mercedes-Benz, and an international panel of 45 journalists from six European countries voted the 450SEL Car of the Year for 1973, on account of its 'outstanding and well-balanced qualities, such as safety, ride comfort and performance'. To be sure, the award went to the European-specification model, and not to the strangled Federal car, which at this time had not been launched, but from now on it became almost commonplace to wonder: was a Rolls-Royce or a Mercedes-Benz the Best Car in the World?

The 350SEL and 280SEL

Once the long-wheelbase W116 shell was in production, it was only a matter of time before it would be offered with the two smaller engines. The 350SEL became available in the autumn of 1973 for the 1974 season, but the 280SEL did not reach the showrooms until early 1974. Indeed, there may have been no

Bird's-eye view of the engine installation of a 280SE (left) and a 350SE (right). The shorter length of the V8 block considerably eased the packaging job.

280SEL at all without the panic about large engines consequent upon the Arab-Israeli War and the ensuing oil shortage. The history of the long-wheelbase models represents in microcosm the reactions to that shortage: after an initial panic in which manufacturers and buyers favoured smaller engines, demand for the larger engines was restored, and the 280SEL became not only the lowest-selling long-wheelbase W116, but also the lowest-selling S-class model of all. Only 4,266 were built in seven

A W116 at speed. Although justifiably popular in every market in which they have been sold, these cars were bred for covering long distances at very high speed and in great comfort. Consequently, their qualities are never better demonstrated than in Western Germany, with its sophisticated autobahn network, much of it, at the time of writing, still free from unrealistic speed limits.

seasons of production. The 350SEL was never exactly a high-volume seller, either, but there never seemed to be any shortage of customers for the 450SEL, which was the most expensive and least fuel-efficient model of all!

The first North American variants of the W116 became available for the 1974 calendar-year. To meet regulations then in force, they had twin circular headlamps in place of the rectangular flush-lensed installations on European cars, and the front foglights so displaced were slung untidily below the bumpers. These were now of the impact-absorbing type to meet the latest regulations, and added no fewer than 10 inches to the length of the car, together with even more weight, although this was minimized by the use of aluminium in their construction. Emissions-control gear and the need to run on lead-free fuel ensured that performance of the North American cars was poorer than that of their European counterparts, and fuel consumption was higher. The 3½-litre engine was no longer certified for the US market, and so only the 280S and the two 4½-litre models were made available at first. Power losses in the Federal 4½-litre engine were such that it could happily use the same gearbox as the 3½-litres, instead of the uprated box necessary in the European-specification 450 models.

In the aftermath of the Arab-Israeli War, the big car became anti-social for a time, and the 1974 calendar-year figures show a dramatic decline in total sales of 350SE and 450SE models. 280S sales increased significantly, however, as might have been expected, and a healthy demand for the 4½-litre cars in the US also led to an increase in 450SEL sales. Daimler-Benz had begun making cars to customer order without boot-lid badging in 1972, and it was now that the fashion became more widespread among S-class buyers: as 2.8-litre and 4½-litre cars were almost indistinguishable to look at, the wealthy man who ran an unbadged 4½-litre car ran less risk of arousing resentment among those who were not sure whether his W116 was really a more economical 2.8-litre model! Later, the process worked in reverse, of course. Those unable to afford a 450SE could buy an unbadged 280S and allow the neighbours to think there was a 4½-litre V8 under the bonnet!

CHAPTER 5

A new flagship

The 450SEL 6.9

By 1974 the trend away from the most powerful and thirsty cars was well established, yet the very next W116 to reach the showrooms seemed to go against everything which the fuel crisis represented, for it had the biggest engine seen in any postwar Mercedes-Benz. In fact, the 450SEL 6.9 which appeared at the 1975 Frankfurt Motor Show had undoubtedly been held over until public reaction to the fuel crisis had stabilized. By the beginning of 1975, the trend back towards big engines was already discernible, however, and Stuttgart's directors authorized production of the new car.

The 450SEL 6.9 was inspired by the same philosophy which had lain behind the 300SEL 6.3, the model which it replaced after a gap of three years. In other words, it coupled the largest and most powerful passenger car engine with the bodyshell of the S-class flagship saloon to produce a Q-car, an ultra-high-performance saloon which looked scarcely different to the standard S-class model. The extra weight of the W116 bodyshell as compared to the superseded W109, plus the power-sapping Federal emissions-control regulations, had meant, however, that even the 6.3-litre V8 of the low-volume 600 limousine was not man enough for the job. Stuttgart considered that there was no point in building the car at all if it could not at least equal the performance of the old 300SEL 6.3, so the engineers went for more power and torque in an enlarged version of the big V8.

As early as 1969, 6.9-litre versions of the W100 had been tried experimentally in examples of the 300SEL 6.3 intended for competition use, and the Daimler-Benz engineers already knew how far they could go and still keep the engine both reliable and docile at low speeds. For the W116, therefore, the W100 engine was bored-out from 103mm to 107mm, which took the cylinder capacity up to 6,834cc. In order to fit this relatively tall engine beneath the low W116 bonnet, a dry-sump lubrication system was specified.

However, more power and torque were not the only aims of the 6.9-litre engine, and on it were tested several features which would later find their way into the lesser models. Thus, it became the first passenger car engine from Stuttgart to use Bosch's new mechanically-controlled K-Jetronic fuel injection system, which was not only cheaper to make than the electronically-controlled D-Jetronic, but also easier to adapt to meet varying emissions-control standards. Similarly, a good deal of thought had gone into servicing requirements, and the factory claimed that their new engine should run for up to 50,000 miles without any more than filter, oil and plug changes. On the earlier V8s, the rocker arms in the valve-gear needed periodic re-adjustment to maintain the correct clearances, but in the 6.9-litre engine, oil was fed under pressure to the fulcrum points of these rockers to give them a self-adjusting function similar to that of hydraulic tappets. A side benefit, of course, was that the engine ran more quietly. Finally, a new type of head gasket made by Reinz-Repa eliminated the need for retorquing the heads after the initial running-in period.

In the European 450SEL 6.9, the engine put out 286bhp (36bhp more than its 6.3-litre parent) and a staggering 405lb/ft of torque at 3,000rpm. Driving through the W3B 050 three-speed automatic transmission to a very high final drive of 2.65:1, and putting its power down to the road through a ZF limited-slip differential and even fatter tyres than on the 4½-litres, this gave precisely the kind of performance which was wanted. Daimler-

The best way to distinguish between a 450SEL 6.9 and an 'ordinary' 450SEL from the front is by looking at the tyres. The big-engined car was supplied with wider 215/70 VR 14 rubber.

Benz claimed a very conservative 140mph top speed, but a number of motoring journalists enjoyed themselves to the full in finding out that the actual top speed was much nearer 150mph! In that respect, the 450SEL 6.9 out-performed the old 300SEL 6.3, but it was so much heavier that not even all that torque could keep standing-start times at their former levels. Even though 0-60mph in under 7½ seconds sounds quick, the 300SEL 6.3 had been a whole second quicker; and the detoxed Federal cars which arrived in 1977 were, of course, even slower.

The extra weight of the 450SEL 6.9 was not only attributable to the heavier W116 bodyshell, however. The car was further distinguished from its lesser brethren by a sophisticated new suspension system which Stuttgart was considering for future use in other models, and indeed it did appear as an option for certain models of the 1979 W126 S-class range. The new suspension was a departure for Mercedes-Benz in that it was a hydro-pneumatic system similar in principle to that used by Citroen for many years. In place of the coil springs of the standard W116, it had a pressurized cylinder filled with nitrogen over each wheel and oil-filled struts which incorporated gas dampers. An engine-driven pump kept the nitrogen system under pressure and topped up by a reservoir which ensured that the system still worked after the engine had been switched off. The system was automatically self-levelling, and ride height could be adjusted even while the car was in motion to give up to 1½ inches of extra ground clearance. Where it scored over the air suspension used in the W109s was that it was less prone to suffer from leaks or faulty balance-valves; and where it scored over the

From the back, the badging made it easier to tell; but some customers ordered their cars without badges!

superb Citroen system was in its retention of the handling qualities offered by the standard W116 suspension in combination with a more supple ride. Like the suspension, the braking system with its 'stepped' master-cylinders was also under consideration for future use. The 'stepped' arrangement consisted of tandem master-cylinders with different bore sizes. The idea was that if the front hydraulic circuit failed, the different bore diameter of the cylinder serving the rear brake lines would automatically compensate by increasing the braking effort there, and thus the loss in braking efficiency would be minimized.

With all this sophisticated and limited-production technology on board, the 450SEL 6.9 was a fearsomely expensive car (nearly as costly as a Rolls-Royce Silver Shadow saloon), but nevertheless it sold quite well at a steady 1,500-2,000 units a year until it was withdrawn in 1979. It was a particular favourite with those wealthy clients who thought they needed an armour-plated car, as its awesome reserves of power and torque ensured that it remained a rapid machine even when heavily-laden with armour plate. Not surprisingly, it was very often found without identifying badges on the boot-lid.

In the meantime, development had continued on the other S-class models. The 4½-litre engine was fitted with K-Jetronic injection from October 1975, shortly after the arrival of the 6.9-litre, and the 3½-litres were brought into line in January 1976. For 1976, equipment levels had been upgraded across the range, with items like a cruise control, rear headrests, heated seats and a self-seeking radio with stereo tape deck becoming part of the specification. The 280SE was introduced to North America for

Under the bonnet of a 450SEL 6.9. The engine was only marginally bigger than the 4½-litre V8, leaving room for the hydro-pneumatic suspension equipment. Nevertheless, there was not much space wasted in there!

the first time, no doubt to offset the trend against big-engined cars. Then for 1977 came improved air conditioning units with a larger evaporator and increased blower volume, while the 450SE disappeared from the American market and the frontal appearance of the remaining US models (the 280S excepted) was tidied-up as the foglights were recessed into the bumpers. Yet the most important 1977 changes were to the emissions-control equipment of North American cars, and they demonstrated how Stuttgart was getting to grips with the problems of US legislation. Since 1975, Californian cars had been fitted with catalytic converters in the exhaust manifolds, and now that the rest of America also required such an installation, the converters were resited under the floor with a heat shield, thus reducing under-bonnet temperatures and increasing the life-span of the converters. There was a new vacuum transducer for exhaust gas metering, and on the V8 engines the air injection pump was replaced by a pulsating air induction system which connected to secondary passages in the cylinder heads. Not only did it reduce power drain, but it was also quieter in operation than the air pump had been.

1977: The 300SD

The 300SD was the final variant of the W116 S-class to be introduced. Even though it was only intended for the North American market, Daimler-Benz showed it proudly at Frankfurt in 1977, probably to remind European customers that, the 450SEL 6.9 notwithstanding, the company really was taking a responsible attitude to the fuel crisis! For the 300SD would run up to 25 miles on a gallon of fuel. This, though, was an S-class car with a difference, because its engine ran on diesel.

There was probably no way in which the 300SD could ever have gained acceptance in Europe, where the attitude persisted that diesel power is for economy cars and taxis, and not at all suitable for luxury cars. In North America, though, where the 300SD became available for the 1978 calendar-year, legislation had forced motorists to come to terms with the need for fuel efficiency in a way which Europe had not experienced, and even Cadillac were thinking about a diesel-engined model (can anyone imagine a diesel-powered Rolls-Royce?). The 300SD therefore gained rapid acceptance in North America, and in fact sold very well indeed during its four seasons of production.

Daimler-Benz were probably better-placed than any other manufacturer to notice how sales of diesel-powered passenger cars in North America shot up after the Arab-Israeli War in 1973. If the large and thirsty petrol-engined car was losing sales and becoming increasingly irrelevant in America anyway, thanks to that country's 55mph speed limit, the best way of remaining in the large-car market there was likely to be to offer a large car with a diesel engine. Problem number one, though, was that all the existing diesel passenger car units from Stuttgart had been designed for much smaller and lighter cars, and the W116 was a particularly heavy vehicle.

The problem is most easily understood by comparing the power outputs of the biggest Mercedes-Benz diesel passenger car engine and of the smallest petrol engine available in the W116

The W116 was a favourite as the basis of an armour-plated car, especially in its bigger-engined forms, where the power and torque could easily cope with the extra weight of the armour plate. Rapport Rental in London took this example of the Rapport Armalite conversion into their exclusive hire fleet—after patching up the bullet-holes in the outer skin panel and glass, of course.

The conversion specialists Crayford, in England, made a small number of these highly expensive and exclusive estate cars. The general proportions of the body were most attractive.

shell. The five-cylinder 2,998cc OM617 diesel unit (then available in the 240D 3.0) produced no more than 80bhp, while the carburetted 2,746cc petrol unit of the W116 280S put out exactly twice as much in European form and around 120bhp with full emissions-control gear. Some performance loss might be acceptable in a diesel W116, but power losses of this magnitude were certainly not going to attract the customers. Obviously, a more powerful diesel engine was needed.

A six-cylinder diesel engine was planned for the future, but there was no chance that it would be ready in time (it actually appeared in the W124 300D in 1985), so a stop-gap had to be found. In the wake of the oil crisis had emerged a new vogue for increasing engine power without increasing fuel consumption by the use of exhaust-driven turbochargers, and it was in America, hardest-hit by the effects of the oil crisis, that the most advanced technology was available. Stuttgart's engineers decided to go down that road, and turned to the Los Angeles firm of Garrett AiResearch when they began work on turbocharging their most powerful existing diesel engine in January 1976. By March, the 200bhp C-111 record-breaker with its turbocharged five-cylinder diesel engine had been built to demonstrate how well things were going, although there was never any intention to put such highly-tuned engines into production cars. When the 300SD became available in late 1977, its OM617 engine had no more than 115bhp – but that represented a nett gain of 35bhp, or nearly 44%, over the unblown engine. A silk purse had indeed

The 450SEL 6.9 engine, featuring dry-sump lubrication, hydraulic valve clearance adjustment, and mechanically operated fuel injection.

been made out of what might otherwise have been a sow's ear, for the 300SD would out-accelerate a North American 280SE, and could achieve 110mph when fully extended. Performance could have been better with a manual gearbox, but Americans love their automatics and so the four-speed Daimler-Benz autobox was the only available transmission option.

Rather more had been done to the OM617 than simply bolting on the Garrett TA 0301 turbocharger, however. The turbocharger itself had been modified to meet Daimler-Benz's exacting requirements and, instead of a simple dump valve to relieve pressure if the wastegate became overloaded, there was a complex system designed to protect the engine. Normal boost was 11psi, but if pressure reached 14/15psi, the dump valve would open while a linkage reduced fuel flow. This in turn would lower the pressure and temperature in the cylinders and also reduce the exhaust gases flowing through the turbocharger, so that boost was also cut back until things returned to normal. To cope with the greater strains imposed by the turbocharger, the basic engine had also been modified. The cylinder-head had redesigned prechambers and new pin-type glow plugs, a new head gasket was specified, and all the valves had thicker heads while the exhausts were sodium-cooled. Crankshaft, con-rods and thrust bearing were all tougher, and a new oil pump delivered nearly twice as much oil as that on the unblown 3-litre diesel. The

For the 1978 season a 300SD model was added to the W116 range, primarily for the US market. As indicated by the script on the boot-lid, the five-cylinder diesel engine had been fitted with a turbo-charger (by Garrett). On later cars more discreet badging was adopted for the S-class turbodiesel.

pistons were now cooled by oil squirted from jets at the bottom of each cylinder; oil was injected into one side of each piston where it was retained briefly in cast-in passages before discharging on the other side, thanks to the piston's rocking motion.

Turbo lag has always been the bane of the turbocharged car, but the combination of sophisticated engineering, automatic transmission and the 300SD's great weight seemed to mask the usual shortcoming. Lag was only really noticeable under full acceleration from rest, and then only as a 3-second hesitation. Once the turbocharger cut in at around 2,000rpm, the 300SD would just surge smoothly onward. Strangely, though, there was no boost gauge on the dashboard, where only an idle-speed adjuster and glow-plug lamp gave any indication that this was not a petrol-engined W116.

Outside, the story was the same, and the 300SD looked like any other North American standard-wheelbase W116. Invisibly, though, it had actually undergone a rigorous weight-trimming programme in order to qualify it for the under-4,000lb US Government certification class. The front bulkhead was of aluminium, as were the bonnet and (later) the boot-lid. A smaller fuel tank, made possible by the remarkable fuel economy, also saved some weight. Nevertheless, equipment levels were high, to help promote the up-market image, and such items as air conditioning and alloy wheels were standard. In just one respect did its appointments let down the Mercedes-Benz tradition – the great, garish, red-and-silver 'Turbodiesel' badge on the boot-lid of the original cars was a severe lapse of taste which had come about presumably at the behest of the American importers. Fortunately, it was replaced during 1978 by the more discreet badge seen on the W123 Turbodiesel models.

1979: Production ends

By the end of the 1970s, the W116's great weight ran contrary to the latest design trends, and the drag factor of its admittedly bulky body was unfashionably high. W116 production ceased in the autumn of 1979, although the cars remained available in

The 300SD's engine involved much more than adding a Garrett turbocharger to the standard five-cylinder diesel engine. The increased operating temperatures, a 44% increase in power and 37% more torque called for extensive internal modifications.

Velour upholstery, fitted as standard on the top S-class models, was also a popular extra-cost choice of buyers of less expensive W116 saloons. This is a 280SE with the luxurious trim.

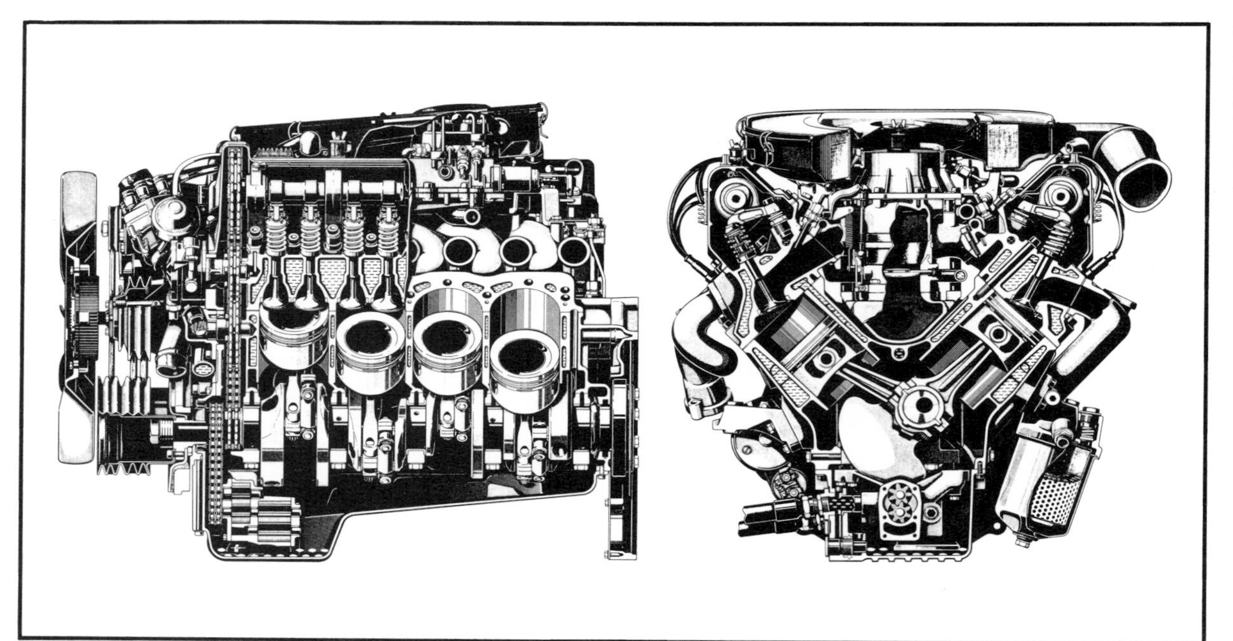

The M100 6.9-litre engine exposed. Based on the earlier 6.3-litre V8, the extra displacement was found by increasing the cylinder bore from 103 to 107mm, the 95mm stroke remaining unchanged.

showrooms outside Germany until the middle of the following year, and stocks of some US models had deliberately been built up to help sales continue into 1981. At home, though, the new lightweight S-class model had become available. The W126 was to prove a worthy successor to the W116, a design for the 1980s that would enhance the Mercedes-Benz reputation even further.

CHAPTER 6

Versatility of a theme

The W123 models from 200 to 280E

It is always tempting to wonder why a manufacturer feels compelled to replace a highly-successful product, and many commentators did query the need for Daimler-Benz to replace the W114/115 models in 1976. At that stage, the range had been by far the most successful ever produced at Stuttgart, and demand was still outstripping supply. The fact of the matter, though, was the Mercedes-Benz engineers knew they could do even better; and so the W123 range was introduced.

In the planning for this new range, the question of high-volume production had been carefully considered. The greater the production volume, as so many other manufacturers had demonstrated, the lower the quality of the finished product tended to be, and the Directors of Daimler-Benz were adamant that there should be no reduction in the traditionally high standards of their vehicles. So the introduction of greater mechanization to enable cars to be produced more quickly was carefully planned to ensure that quality was actually improved. The W123 lines installed at Sindelfingen incorporated the very latest and most sophisticated robots to perform 99% of the body welds without the need for human intervention; the machines achieved greater consistency and uniformity than human welders ever could, and those members of the work-force displaced by the machinery were redeployed to deal with the important (and psychologically more rewarding) hand-finishing tasks on the trim and interior. Not only did W123 production eventually outstrip that of the W114/115 range, but the quality of the vehicles was even higher.

Engineering development of the W123, however, began much earlier than the restructuring of the Sindelfingen assembly lines, and the first thoughts of its designers were committed to paper in 1968 – only a year after the production launch of the models it was to replace. As with the W114/115 cars, both four and six-cylinder versions were planned, although a single type-designation was this time considered adequate to cover both. A new family of engines was already being considered for introduction in the W114/115 models mid-way through their production life, and so the W123 would naturally begin life with these power units. As before, both coupe and long-wheelbase variants would also be built, but this time there were plans to expand the range even further by offering a factory-produced estate body as soon as spare production capacity was available. In addition, the floorpan and running-gear would be made available to the specialist conversion companies for the fitment of commercial bodywork. By offering such a diversity of variants, Daimler-Benz hoped to sell the W123 in sufficiently large quantities to amortize the huge costs which would be incurred in making this range even more sophisticated than its predecessors.

The engineering department, under Hans Scherenberg, set itself a number of design aims for the W123. First, the new car should be safer than its predecessors. Second, it should satisfy, and preferably stay ahead of, the new legislation which many countries were beginning to introduce in the late 1960s to govern motor vehicle design. The third aim of general refinement and technical improvement was only to be expected, but the fourth aim was especially interesting, and that was to improve the ease of repair and servicing. Long before most other manufacturers, Stuttgart had recognized that the car was becoming increasingly complex, and that if servicing tasks were not eventually to pass

The neat lines of the W123 saloons were to serve Daimler-Benz well, enabling this series to remain in production to the mid-1980s as the company's best-selling range. This is a 200 which, like other models below the 280, featured circular headlamps until front-end styling was standardized across the range in 1982.

beyond the ability of the Third World mechanic, a programme of simplification was going to be necessary alongside those of technical progress.

The safety improvements in the W123 incorporated both active and passive elements. On the active side, revisions to the suspension brought handling improvements. The new model had wider tracks than its predecessors, although its rear suspension was unchanged except in detail from the semi-trailing-arm layout of the W114/115, which Stuttgart *still* insisted on calling diagonal swing-axles! At the front, though, the new anti-dive

This is the 230E version of the W123 saloon, which replaced the earlier carburettor-equipped four-cylinder 2.3-litre model. This was the first time Daimler-Benz had offered a fuel-injected version of a four-cylinder petrol engine.

suspension layout first seen in the W116 S-class saloons was introduced, together with the zero-offset steering geometry which added so much to stability. As in the W116, the suspension was bolted up directly to the bodyshell rather than carried on a subframe, but power steering was only an option which was standardized on the more expensive models. Brakes were discs all round – the W114/115 range had used drums at the rear – with servo-assistance and a split hydraulic circuit as standard. In addition, the ingenious 'stepped' master-cylinder arrangement first seen on the 450SEL 6.9 was specified. The entire braking system was common to both four and six-cylinder variants, so that not only were production costs saved, but brake pad life on the lower-performance models was increased.

Passive safety improvements began with the construction of the bodyshell which, following the lead of the W116, had a stronger passenger cage and weaker front and rear crumple zones than had been previous practice. Roll-over stiffness had been improved through careful attention to the design of the window pillars, which were nevertheless thinner than before in the interests of better visibility, and side-impact protection was greater thanks to doors designed to collapse progressively and to rigid under-floor cross-members. At the front, dimples on the inner edges of the main side-members controlled their collapse under impact, while the bulkhead area where the side-members met the floor was reinforced to limit the extent of impact damage. At the rear, the spare wheel was mounted S-class fashion below the boot floor, to help reduce damage in a rear-end shunt. As Mercedes-Benz promotional material put it, limiting the damage caused by an accident not only protected the occupants but also made the car cheaper to repair afterwards.

A few examples of the many passive safety features of the W123 will reveal the impressive attention to detail which had gone into the design. Research at Stuttgart had shown that most frontal collisions involved a diagonal impact rather than a head-on crash, and so the steering column was designed to deflect sideways as well as to telescope. The parking-brake release linkage, formerly a rod, was now a chain which could not be forced into the passenger-cabin under impact, and the inward-pointing struc-

The neat but functional dashboard of a W123 280 or 280E. Just visible below the steering wheel on the left is the parking-brake pedal.

tural flange on the screen pillars of the W114/115 cars had now been turned through 90° to point away from the W123's occupants. Details like the counter-balanced door locks and the handles which pulled rather than pressed were inherited from the W107s and W116s.

Inside, there was padding in abundance, with a flexible bolster at knee height to protect the front seat occupants. The inboard seat belt mountings were on the seats, so that a constant belt position was ensured regardless of the seat setting and, yet another tiny detail, the return springs for the pedals were moved forward of the pedal hangars in order to be as far removed as possible from contact with the driver's legs. Instrumentation followed the lines already laid down by the W107 and W116 models, but control of lighting was now transferred from the multi-function column stalk to a rotary switch on the dashboard. Speedometers for US-market cars were marked for the first time in both miles and kilometres per hour, in anticipation of the proposed metrication of that country. Although floor-mounted gear-levers were standard, cars with automatic transmission could still be specified with a column-mounted selector lever.

Styling of the W123 was very much in the W116 idiom, and the smaller car was in many respects a scaled-down version of the S-class, but with a more pronounced rake front-to-rear and a much lighter appearance overall. Without a doubt, it was one of the most successful postwar designs from the company, being elegant, restrained and tasteful and yet far from anonymous. Incorporated in the styling were some intriguing touches, like the doors which overlapped their sills and thus kept clean the area most likely to come into contact with the clothes of passengers boarding or alighting from the vehicle. Similarly, the discreet flash of trim at the base of the rearmost window pillars was not purely a cosmetic addition, but actually concealed a panel join to make the replacement of a damaged rear wing that much simpler and cheaper.

During assembly, the engines of the W123 cars were lowered into the bodyshells, whereas previous practice had been to lower

Right-hand-drive cars, however, were fitted with an umbrella-type handbrake protruding from the facia and released with a twist action.

the bodies on to the engines and running-gear. As the bonnets were already attached when the W123 shells met up with their engines, this meant that the bonnet had to be openable to a fully vertical position – which of course helped considerably in major servicing tasks. A special catch on the hinges released the bonnet to allow it to rise beyond the normal 'open' position. All the W123 shells were also subjected during assembly to a five-stage rust-proofing process, beginning with the application of a zinc phosphate to the bodyshell and ending with the application of a plasticized vinyl bolstered by a petroleum-based preservative which was sprayed on to the underside and protected not only this, but also the engine compartment, driveshaft, fuel and brake lines, and the insides of the hollow body structures. The early W114/115 models had gained themselves an unenviable reputation for rusting, but it is a rare sight indeed to spot a rusty W123.

The four-cylinder saloons – 200, 230 and 230E

Although pilot-production of the initial pair of four-cylinder W123 models was undertaken in July 1975, full production did not begin until the following February, and the cars were not publicly launched until the Geneva Show in March, when the full nine-model W123 range was shown. Cars became available immediately in European markets, but the USA had to wait until early 1977 before the new 230 arrived, and never did receive the 200 model.

Sales of the W115 models had been so strong to the very last that the company decided to keep the old models in production while W123 production built up – and indeed, the same overlap was arranged for other W123 variants. The W115 200 and 230/4 accordingly remained in production until December 1976, and both were available in the showrooms until well into 1977. Nevertheless, W123 production built up rapidly and the total production of four-cylinder models in 1976 exceeded that of the W115 cars by more than two to one.

The W123 200 and 230 shared their engines with the W115 cars, although minor changes to improve fuel economy had resulted in a change to the quoted power figures, and the 200's 1,988cc M115 unit was now quoted as developing 94bhp at 4,800rpm (down from 95bhp at 5,000rpm), while the 230's big-bore 2,307cc version of the same engine had 109bhp at 4,800rpm instead of 110bhp at 5,200rpm. The detoxed Federal and Californian engines were, of course, less powerful, and low-compression versions were also made for countries where high-octane fuel was not available. All variants of both engines had a single Stromberg carburettor. Although there were marketing variations from country to country, all the four-cylinder W123s could be had with the same four-speed synchromesh or four-speed torque converter automatic gearboxes as their predecessors, and axle ratios were also unchanged.

Like all the smaller-engined W123s and the diesel models, the 200 and 230 had circular headlamps and foglamps behind a rectangular glass panel. North American 230s had the impact-absorbing bumpers necessary in that market, but these were much better integrated into the overall styling than on previous models, and added only a few inches to the total length. Equipment levels were fairly basic, in standard Stuttgart fashion, but the wide range of optional extras included such items as power-assisted steering, vacuum central locking, alloy wheels, electric windows, an electric sunroof, metallic paint, leather upholstery and hydro-pneumatic self-levelling rear suspension. Some markets only imported cars with certain options fitted; thus all 230s for the UK had both automatic transmission and power-assisted steering. The 230, but not the 200, was also offered as the basis for specialist conversions such as ambulances, when it was fitted with 15-inch wheels and the lower 3.92:1 axle ratio of the 200 models.

Minor improvements were made over the next few years, but the next major changes came just too late for the Frankfurt Show in 1979, when all models were given new engines and the manual gearboxes were replaced with transmissions of a new design. The two new engines, development of which had been the responsibility of Dr Derndinger, reflected the same considerations which had underpinned the development programme for 1979's light-alloy V8s. For a start, lighter construction was employed, and the engines were physically smaller than before, with reduced oil and water capacities. Greater fuel efficiency was achieved through cross-flow cylinder heads incorporating hemispherical combustion chambers (as usual, both were OHC designs), but the engines were also much more powerful than their predecessors. Cylinder capacities, at 1,997cc and 2,299cc, were similar to those of the old units, with the larger engine again sharing the stroke of the smaller one but having bigger bores. While the 109bhp 200 unit still had a single Stromberg carburettor, the 136bhp 2.3-litre came with Bosch fuel injection, and the car it powered therefore gained an 'E' in its model-name. The W123 230E thus became the first fuel-injected four-cylinder Mercedes-Benz, all previous fuel-injected models having had six or eight cylinders.

The M102 engines, as they were designated, also needed less routine maintenance, for servicing intervals had been extended from 6,000 to 12,000 miles. Both reflected Stuttgart's preoccupation with reducing driver fatigue, for their greater power outputs meant that they expended less effort than the engines they replaced to produce the same result and were thus effectively quieter. Publicity material further suggested that the addition of eight counterweights to the five main bearings and the consequent smoother running were also part of the programme to reduce driver fatigue, but it might have been more honest to admit that they were really an attempt to refine the big 'fours' and to keep them competitive with the silky-smooth 'six' in BMW's rival 3-series saloons. Fitting North American emissions-control gear to the M102s would certainly have robbed them of some of this new-found refinement, and it may be for that reason that neither engine was certificated for sale in the USA; after 1980, therefore, no more four-cylinder W123s were available in that market.

The automatic gearboxes were unchanged for 1980, but with the two new engines came a new four-speed manual gearbox, similar in gearing to the older units, but lighter in weight thanks to die-cast aluminium construction, and smoother in action. Axle gearing of the 200 remained as before, but the 230E's greater torque was able to cope with a higher 3.58:1 axle, which made for both more restful cruising and better fuel consumption. As had occurred during the W115/W123 changeover four years earlier,

Interior of one of the 1983-season 'face-lift' models, with their new trim material, smaller headrests and redesigned rear bench seat.

There has never yet been a saloon from Stuttgart with a less than enormous boot. Yes, those cases *will* all go in . . .

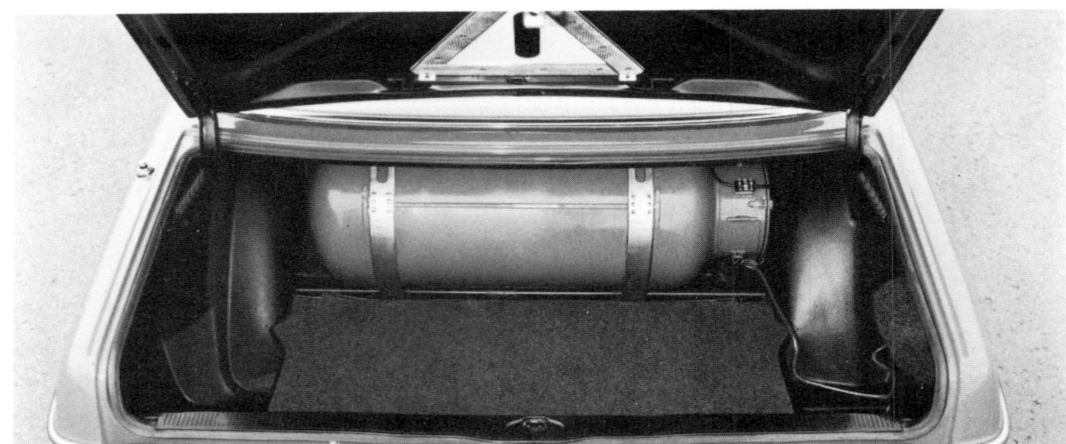

. . . but there is a first time for everything. From 1982, the 200 could be bought with an LPG installation, the tank for which occupied 30% of the normal boot space. The car could operate on either liquified gas or premium-grade petrol.

The LPG-equipped car could be recognized by its extra fuel filler. It never sold in large quantities.

there was actually a considerable overlap of production, with the new models gradually ousting the old from the production lines, but both being built side-by-side for a time. The pilot batches of both new models had been built in October 1979, but the old 200 carried on until August 1980 and the 230 just over a year longer until September 1981, which reflected the greater sales it had always achieved.

The first two-and-a-half years' production of the M102-engined cars saw a number of revisions to their specifications. An improved heating and ventilating system arrived in August 1980, and in the rare cases where air conditioning was fitted, it was of the new type introduced in the W126 S-class. August 1980 also saw the introduction of the new ABS anti-lock braking system as an option. The autumn 1981 Energy Concept revisions were minimal on the four-cylinder cars, however, as the M102 engines had already been designed with maximum fuel economy in mind. The 200 engine remained unchanged, but the 230E unit was fitted with an overrun fuel cut-off mechanism and an improved transistorized ignition unit, while its idling speed was lowered. The new five-speed gearbox associated with the Energy Concept changes became available on both models from February 1982, and then, from spring that year, some markets were offered a 200 which would run on both petrol and LPG, the extra tank for the latter being installed in the boot. Yet these changes, while important in themselves, meant less to the company's marketing men than did the fillip given by the facelift which affected all the 1983-season W123 models.

As far as the 200 and 230E were concerned, the most obvious change was that they now gained the rectangular headlamps and foglamps previously specified only on the top six-cylinder models. Like all the W123s, the four-cylinders also received all-black air intake grilles ahead of the windscreen, and redesigned mouldings on the front and rear roof pillars. There was remote electric adjustment for the passenger door mirror and an interior light delay, while an economy gauge was fitted in line with the cross-range Energy Concept improvements initiated in 1981. Yet the appointments had not been neglected in this drive for fuel economy, and there was more wood veneer inside, better seat fabric material with longitudinal pleating, reshaped back seats giving more kneeroom and a better seating position, and redesigned headrests which were less obstructive than before. The range of optional extras was also extended, and power-assisted steering became standard, although this did not affect all markets; in the UK, for example, PAS had always been standard on the 230/230E, and standard since September 1978 on the 200.

The six-cylinder saloons – 250, 280 and 280E

The pilot batches of the three six-cylinder saloons were built at

1980 saw the arrival of two new M102 four-cylinder engines, this being the 2-litre unit, as fitted to the 200.

the same time as the pilot-build four-cylinder W123s in July 1975, but although full production of the 280 and 280E models began in December, volume assembly of the 250 models did not begin until April 1976. Nevertheless, examples of all three models were on display at Geneva the previous month.

The delay in production of the 2½-litre cars was caused by the slow build-up of engine stocks, for these cars were the only models of the 1976 W123 range to have a new engine. Known as the M123, this was a 2,525cc OHC design, which put out a disappointingly unrefined 129bhp at 5,500rpm. The engines in the 280 and 280E were the 2,746cc DOHC M110 units, which gave 156bhp in single-Solex form and 177bhp with Bosch K-Jetronic fuel injection. Of these, only the 280E was sold in the USA, where it had impact-absorbing bumpers and circular headlamps in place of the rectangular units which distinguished the European six-cylinders. The 250 was also offered in long-wheelbase form as a basis for ambulance and other conversions, and in all these extended forms it had 15-inch wheels, although the 3.69:1 axle ratio of the standard saloon remained unchanged. All the 2.8-litre models wore low-profile 195/70 HR 14 tyres, and shared the same 3.54:1 axle ratio. Gearboxes in all cases were identical to those of the four-cylinder cars, until 1981's Energy Concept changes saw the W4A 025 automatic transmission replaced by the W4A 040 type previously seen only in the W126 S-class cars. This had smoother down-changes, was more sensitive than the old type to part-throttle kickdown and would hold kickdown to higher engine speeds, but was also programmed to change up as early as possible as a fuel-saving

The 2½-litre six-cylinder M123 engine was new for the W123 series and never found another home. The 250 models had round headlamps.

measure. At idle, second gear engaged automatically to reduce 'creep', but first gear was instantly selected when the accelerator was depressed.

Equipment levels in the six-cylinder models were higher than in the cheaper W123s, and these differentials were emphasized in certain markets such as the UK, where the 250 had both automatic transmission and power-assisted steering as standard, while the 280E added tinted glass and rear head restraints to its standard specification. In fact, PAS was standard for all markets on the 280 and 280E, but was not standardized in all markets until August 1978 on the 250. From November 1977, a 3.58:1 axle could be specified for the 280, which had little effect on its 115mph top speed, but helped acceleration a little, and then early the following year a raised compression ratio for 280E models put power output up to 185bhp in European form. The 250 was uprated at the 1979 Frankfurt Motor Show, and henceforth had 140bhp thanks to a hotter camshaft, a modified carburettor and a redesigned exhaust system. Production of the 280 stopped in 1981, probably because the car had always been a relatively slow seller, leaving the 250 and 280E in production all the way to the W123s' end in 1984. As for revisions to the trim, appointments and options on the six-cylinder models, these generally ran parallel to the changes made to their lesser brethren throughout the range's life, and of course both 250 and 280E could be had with five-speed manual gearboxes after February 1982.

At the beginning, the 125mph 280E was the best-selling six-cylinder model, but the 250 rapidly supplanted it in this position; as for the 280, that was always a fairly low-volume car and had a short production life. In the USA, the 280E sold in something like nine times the numbers of the four-cylinder 230 model, but even this represented low volumes compared to those of the diesel models.

The diesel saloons – 200D, 220D, 240D, 300D and 300D Turbodiesel

Four diesel saloons were launched with the other W123 models at the Geneva Show in 1976, and all were direct replacements for the previous range of W115 diesels. As with the petrol-engined saloons, the pilot batch had in all cases been run off in July 1975, and full production had begun in February 1976. Sensibly, the '240D 3.0' designation of the European 3-litre diesel had been abandoned, and the new version was known in all markets by the former American designation of 300D.

As before, the four engines were basically of three different types, all with the traditional Mercedes-Benz pre-combuston chambers and a single overhead camshaft. OM615 units went into the 200D and 220D, the former having a 55bhp 1,988cc engine and the latter a long-stroke 2,197cc version of 64bhp. These, of course, were primarily intended as taxis or for fleet users, and the really significant diesel W123s started with the 240D. This had the 2,404cc OM616 engine, which offered rather better acceleration and much greater flexibility thanks to its 99lb/ft maximum torque, even though only 65bhp were available at peak crankshaft speed and the car would show no more than 90mph flat-out. Speed, of course, was not what the 240D was all about. As one advertisement for the US model put it, the 240D 'can take you farther on a tank of fuel than any other car sold in America'. Some very gentle driving was needed to achieve the claimed 633 miles on a tankful of diesel, but the advertisement made its point clearly enough: this was a luxury economy car, designed to win the average owner over from petrol power.

Buyers who wanted more performance with almost comparable economy had to be prepared to find the extra purchase price of a 300D. Here, a 97mph maximum and a 0-60mph time of around 16 seconds made the car generally comparable in performance to a petrol-engined 200, which nevertheless had a 14bhp advantage over the 80bhp put out by the 3-litre diesel engine. This, of course, was the five-cylinder OM617, but it differed from previously-seen versions in that its bore diameter had been slightly reduced to get the capacity under the 3-litre mark which in some territories signalled a tax jump. The 300D thus had 2,998cc instead of the 3,005cc of earlier models with the OM617 engine.

All the diesel models could be had with the same manual or automatic gearboxes as the petrol-engined cars, and axle ratios ranged from 3.92:1 (200D and 220D) through 3.69:1 (240D) to 3.46:1 (300D). These were unchanged even with the 15-inch wheels standard on the two long-wheelbase models offered. Both these – the 240D and 300D – could be had as the basis of specialist conversions, and the standard-wheelbase 240D was also offered to specialist bodybuilders, when it, too, had 15-inch wheels.

The further a buyer was prepared to go up the diesel range, the

Complete with the optional alloy wheels, which did wonders for its appearance, this is the top-of-the-range 280E saloon. Maximum speed was 121mph.

This 280E has the headlamp wash/wipe system fitted to the later cars. Rectangular headlamps like these were originally only fitted to the more expensive W123s, but were standardized across the range in 1982.

Count those injectors! Yes, this is the five-cylinder diesel engine, first introduced in 1974's W115 240D 3.0.

The 300D was initially given the front-end styling of the smaller-engined models in the W123 range.

higher he found the levels of standard equipment, and until the mid-1980 range refinements came in, it was still only the 300D which had a key-start system, all the others having separate ignition, glow-plug and start controls. The 200D and 220D were too spartan and too slow to find many buyers outside the taxi and fleet-user markets, and were not universally available. North America took only the 240D and 300D, both with impact-absorbing bumpers and suitably detoxed engines, while the UK imported only a very few 200D models and concentrated on the two larger-engined cars. PAS was standard in all markets on the 300D, and on all 240Ds sold in the UK and USA. 300Ds also had vacuum central locking as standard, and in the UK they all came with automatic transmission and a windscreen with a graduated band of tinting at the top; but there were many other variations in specification from market to market.

Regardless of what Daimler-Benz publicity in the late 1970s

A 280E with the standard wheels is a comparative rarity on the UK market, where the majority of cars have been equipped with alloy wheels as well as other items of optional equipment.

might have led one to believe, the production changes made to the diesels demonstrate that Stuttgart was acutely conscious of the need for performance improvements. Where performance could not easily be improved, economy was. The 220D ceased production in March 1979, one month after engine changes had put the power output of the 200D up to 60bhp at 4,400rpm and that of the 240D up to 74bhp at the same crankshaft speed. In September, the same changes affected the OM617 engine, and the 300D was now quoted as developing 88bhp at that same 4,400rpm. Performance figures were still pretty leisurely, and even the 300D fell a long way short of a 100mph top speed, but the legendary diesel fuel economy was actually improved. Then,

A four-cylinder W123 with the revised front end incorporating the light units previously reserved for the 2.8-litre models. This car also has optional headlamp wash/wipe equipment.

Following the introduction of the fuel-injected four-cylinder engine the 230E became a highly popular member of the W123 'family', offering an attractive blend of brisk performance with useful fuel economy.

A W123 230E saloon with standard MB-Tex upholstery—very hard-wearing but these days relatively unusual within this price range where cloth trim tends to dominate the market.

in February 1982, a five-speed gearbox was offered for the 200D and the US 240D and 300D models, bringing fuel economy if not performance to even higher levels.

Stuttgart knew that the main hindrance to even higher sales of the diesel models was their lack of performance. Despite North America's 55mph speed limit, this was particularly true in that country, where diesel sales completely outstripped those of the petrol-engined cars. (In the 1980 calendar-year, for example, something like 73% of all Mercedes-Benz passenger cars sold in North America had diesel engines.) So a decision was taken to use the turbocharged 3-litre diesel already developed for the S-class 300SD in a special top-of-the-range diesel W123 for North America only.

The 125bhp engine was introduced first in the W123 estate range, which needed the extra power most on account of the higher payloads it was sometimes asked to carry. Nevertheless, the pilot batch of turbocharged saloons was run off in July 1981, only nine months after estate production commenced, and the vehicle entered full production in September. Unlike the other diesel saloons, it ran on the low-profile tyres of the more expensive petrol-engined cars. The 300TD Turbodiesel (it never had any other name) was an instant success, outselling not only all the other W123 models in North America by 1982, but also every other model in the Mercedes-Benz range. In view of this success, it is perhaps surprising that Stuttgart was not tempted to make the Turbodiesel saloon available in other big diesel markets, such as Italy. Clearly, they still felt that Europe was not ready for a top-flight diesel-powered saloon.

The more familiar cloth upholstery, this time supplied with a 200 saloon equipped with automatic transmission.

American-market model, this time the 300D sedan (saloon).

CHAPTER 7

Coupes and estates

Extending the W123 range

The expected two-door coupe variants of the W123 range appeared in the spring of 1977 and went on sale in the early summer. As before, they were pillarless designs; but this time, the styling was much more successful than that of the W114 coupes had been, with pleasantly integrated lines and none of the heaviness about the rear quarters which had marred the elegance of the earlier cars. Nevertheless, owners of the 'image' models of the W123 range had to be prepared to make certain sacrifices, and these were not only of the financial kind. To achieve the svelte styling on which their image depended so heavily, the coupes had a lower roof-line than the saloons, and sat on a wheelbase which had been shortened by 4 inches. As a result, rear seat passengers were short-changed on both head and legroom. Still, the cars were as well-equipped as a luxury coupe should be, and all came with both low-profile tyres and power-assisted steering as standard. In Europe, though not in America, the coupes all had the rectangular front light units associated with the more expensive saloons.

The Coupes: 230C, 230CE, 280C, 280CE, 300CD and 300CD Turbodiesel

The first pilot-built coupes were 280CE models constructed in October 1976; 230C and 280C models followed in November, and then production of the two 2.8-litre models got under way in April 1977, with the 230C going into production in June. Next on the agenda were the 300CD models, the five-cylinder diesel coupes destined exclusively for North America, which went into production in September 1977 after the pilot batch had been run off in May.

The sales launch of the coupe models was not simultaneous in all markets, and the UK saw none until October 1977, while North America had to wait until early 1978. The two North American models – only the 280CE and 300CD were available there – had the usual impact-absorbing bumpers and round headlamps, plus of course emissions-control equipment and air conditioning as standard, which robbed them of some of the performance which would otherwise have been available. Although manual-transmission coupes *were* made at Sindelfingen, the UK and USA were among those markets which took only automatic models unless to special order.

Despite their high-performance image, the W123 coupes were really no quicker than the equivalent saloon models to which they were mechancially identical, and of course the automatic gearboxes standard in some markets and commonly specified in others ensured that performance was acceptable rather than sparkling. It may have been this which led to a decision to drop the slower carburettor models and to uprate the diesel coupe. Certainly, *Road & Track* had been fairly uncomplimentary about the 300CD, summing it up as 'a car that's all show and no go, an image car with nothing to back up the image'. Stuttgart must have loved that!

The realignment of the coupe range took place in two phases. Both the 230C and 280C ceased production during the first half of 1980, so that they had effectively disappeared from the showrooms by the beginning of the 1981 season, and the new 230CE with the injected version of the 2.3-litre engine arrived at the same time. This left only two petrol-engined coupes in the range for 1981 – the 230CE and 280CE. Then, around a year

Seen here between a 230TE estate and a 230E saloon, the 230CE shows off the rectangular headlamps always fitted to the coupe models.

later, the 300CD was given the turbocharged diesel engine, and the old diesel coupe was withdrawn. Despite the greater appeal of the new higher-performance model, it nevertheless remained exclusive to North America.

More about luxury and image than about performance, the W123 coupes fitted comfortably into the Mercedes-Benz scheme of things; but they did break new ground in two ways. Not since the 170S coupes and cabriolets of 1949-1951 had the up-market two-door variant of a Mercedes-Benz saloon had a four-cylinder engine and never before had such a car been offered with a diesel

These side views of the W123 coupe show off its elegantly harmonious lines and demonstrate the way in which the door and side windows can be wound out of sight to leave the space between front and rear pillars completely unobstructed.

Originally offered as a 230C, the four cylinder-engined coupe became the 230CE on the introduction of the fuel-injected power unit, and like the equivalent saloon model, the extra performance brought with it significantly improved customer appeal.

engine. Both these factors are directly attributable to the effects of the oil crisis in the 1970s, but the mould has been broken and the implications for Mercedes-Benz model policy go far beyond the W123 range's life-span. Of course, it is important not to get these apparently radical changes out of perspective. The best-selling W123 coupe has been the 280CE, the model which best embodies the coupe image of luxury and performance, even though the diesel and Turbodiesel coupes have been best-sellers in the USA. The coupes were the last of the W123 models to remain in production.

In the USA, the coupes had to have round lamps to conform to lighting regulations. This is the diesel-engined 300CD. Note how the impact-absorbing bumpers are far less obstrusive than on earlier designs from Stuttgart.

Front-end accessibility of the 280CE is excellent with the top panel raised, and the insulating mat on the underside of the bonnet is most effective.

Useful pockets are built into the deeply padded doors of the W123 coupes. With the window lowered the only protrusion is the mounting for the interior adjustment of the exterior mirror.

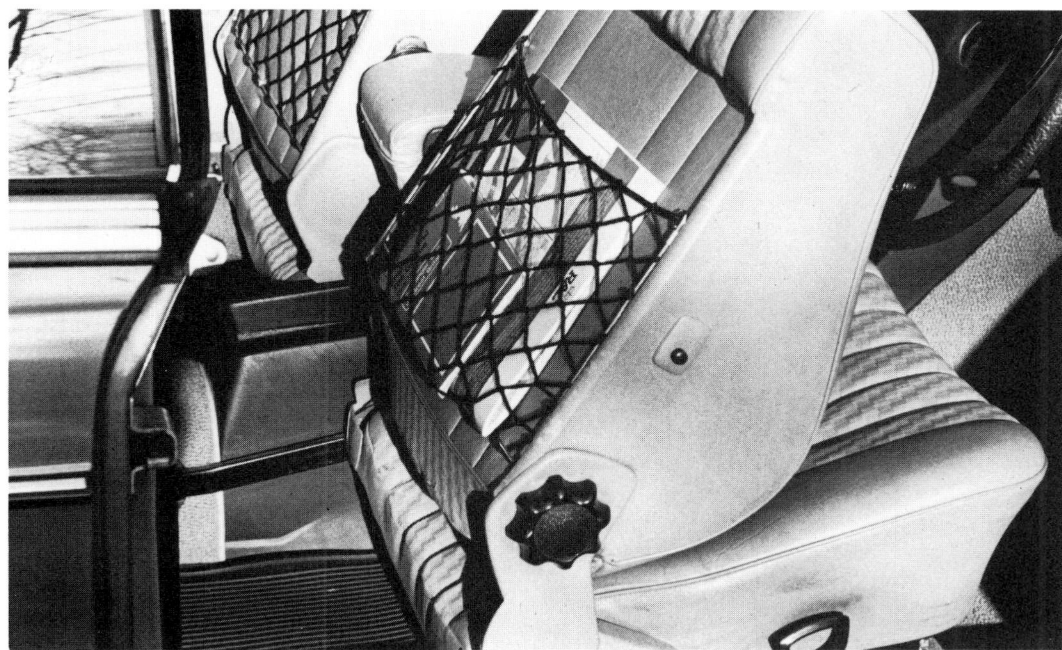

Further handy stowage space is provided in the seat backs of this 280CE, the rear footwells of which have been covered with over-mats.

The 280CE and its four-cylinder equivalent are genuine four-seaters with reasonable rear-passenger legroom. This car features cloth trim, the other trim options being velour or leather.

The luggage compartment of the W123 coupes is generously dimensioned, this particular 280CE having on many occasions performed yeoman service with a heavy load of luggage beneath that red warning triangle!

Exclusive indeed, but expensive, too. This is the 280CE St Tropez Convertible Coupe by Crayford, in England.

The Estates: 200T, 230T, 230TE, 240TD, 250T, 280TE, 300TD and 300TD Turbodiesel

The first estate variants of the W123 went into production during the spring of 1978, and were available in the showrooms for the 1979 season. They consisted of one four-cylinder model (the 230T), two 'sixes' (the 250T and 280TE) and two diesels (the 240TD and 300TD). Like the other W123 models, the estates underwent a range realignment for 1980, with a 200T arriving as the more powerful M102 2-litre engine became available, an injected engine uprating the 230T to a 230TE, and a turbocharger on the 300TD adding some performance to the big diesel which, unlike the saloons and coupes with turbocharged diesel

The American 300TD station wagon (estate) being cornered vigorously, for the benefit of the photographer, no doubt.

power units, was available in some European markets as well as in North America.

The T-range (the T stood for Touristik) represented a major policy change for Stuttgart, as no estate variants had ever been produced in-house before. There was simply no more space at Sindelfingen, and so the assembly lines were installed alongside those for Mercedes-Benz light commercials in the old Borgward factory in Bremen. Initial production estimates were for 10,000 T-series cars in 1978, building up to 24,000 for 1979 and beyond. The new range was thus expected to boost total annual output from Bremen to 60,000 vehicles.

Estate cars based on saloons are rarely a total styling success,

A fully equipped UK-registered 230TE estate, complete with latest-specification front lamps, a manually operated sliding roof and alloy wheels.

but it must be said that the W123 estates were an exception to this general rule. Based on the standard saloon floorpan, albeit strengthened at the rear to give the extra rigidity needed with a large tailgate, they offered no real styling surprises, simply adding a longer roof-line, rear side windows and a single-piece tailgate with a standard wash-wipe system to the saloon shape. The rear sill was at bumper height, which of course had entailed the use of smaller and less comprehensive tail-lamp clusters, while a single reversing lamp and a rear fog-guard lamp were neatly recessed into the bumper. Most impressive of all, perhaps, was the way the W123 estates looked as if they had been designed as a whole, rather than as saloons to which the rear portion had been added as an afterthought.

To maintain trim and handling, the estates had hydro-pneumatic self-levelling as standard at the rear. As an extra precaution, headlamp angle could be adjusted from the dashboard, although it was rare for one of these estates to be so overloaded that the rear end would sag. The actual load-space available in the W123s was adequate rather than particularly large, despite the short-shaft rear shock absorbers with their ingenious cup-and-ball top mountings which allowed angle changes without the need for extra height in the suspension towers which intruded into the rear load-space. Nevertheless, the Mercedes-Benz scored over its more capacious rivals from Volvo, Peugeot and Citroen with pleasing details like the longitudinal runners on the roof, which did not add to the drag coefficient, but could easily (if not quickly) be converted into a roof-rack by the addition of a set of transverse bars normally

The capacious interior of a T-series estate, with the rear seat folded forwards to create maximum load space.

stored in the load compartment. This was a feature soon copied by a number of other manufacturers. The rear seat had a useful one-third/two-thirds split backrest option, so that long loads could be carried without sacrificing all the rear seats, and it was possible to order as an optional extra a rearward-facing bench seat which folded down into the luggage floor when not in use. Other extras included some astronomically expensive aerodynamic trunks for the roof rack, and a detachable unit which combined a dog-guard and a retractable luggage-cover which hooked on to the tailgate and would lift up with it to permit access in a single operation. An optional heavy-load package could also be had, which offered an extra 3 cwt of payload and entailed the fitting of 15-inch wheels.

The T-series cars sold strongly alongside formidable (and cheaper) competition, and by the time they ceased production in 1985, total sales of 200,000 had exceeded the original targets.

Rear view of a W123 estate, in this case the 300TD Turbodiesel with its special badging.

The five-cylinder turbocharged diesel engine was used in the estate before going into other W123 models.

Top model in the estate range, the 280TE offers seemingly effortless performance to go with its generous accommodation.

The W123 in retrospect

Although the W123 was not the most charismatic Mercedes-Benz of the 1970s and 1980s, it *was* the biggest seller, and indeed took from the W114/115 models which it replaced the title of best-selling Mercedes-Benz ever. With a single basic design, Stuttgart had once again been able to embrace the whole spectrum from diesel taxi to high-performance coupe, this time fielding no fewer than 25 basic model variants in nine years, as well as entering a new market sector with the T-series estates. The W123 models were not always class-leaders, but invariably they were finely built, thoroughly engineered and durable. Few other manufacturers of saloons, coupes and estates in the 2 to 3-litre bracket could honestly say that of their products.

The background does help to create the right image, but the T-series is a particularly good-looking car. This example is a 250T.

The fully carpeted and trimmed rear compartment of the 230TE. The spare wheel rests in the trimmed cover on the left.

Wide-opening doors are a feature of all Mercedes-Benz cars and access to the interior of this estate is excellent.

On W123 models the right-hand dial normally occupied by a large clock can be replaced by a combination dial combining a small clock and rev-counter.

Close-up of the cloth upholstery of the car featured in the previous picture. The third rear head restraint emphasizes that this is a true five-seater, to which a further two (rear-facing) seats could be added behind from the options list.

A major attraction of the W123 range is that generous passenger and luggage space is available regardless of the model chosen, leaving only matters of performance and levels of trim and equipment to be tailored to requirements and budgets.

CHAPTER 8

Buying a 1970s Mercedes-Benz

With cost of ownership in mind

With very few exceptions, the models covered in this book were or are still being produced in fairly large numbers, and as the modern Mercedes-Benz proudly upholds the marque's reputation for durability, there is no shortage of cars on the market. That reputation for durability, of course, also means that the cars generally retain their value well. As they were all costly when new, they are likely to be so still, and no enthusiastic would-be owner should start off with any illusions about motoring on the cheap. Buying and running any of the models discussed in this *Collector's Guide* will be an expensive business. All are in high insurance brackets, for the very good reason that rebuilding after an accident is likely to be costly, and even routine spare parts are much more expensive than for more mundane vehicles. It is therefore important to remember that the restoration and maintenance costs of a neglected vehicle are likely to be prohibitive for enthusiasts with shallower pockets. Besides, Mercedes-Benz are fine cars, and few things are sadder than a fine car allowed to deteriorate by an owner who cannot afford to maintain it properly.

That, of course, is the dark side of the picture. More pleasant to relate is that there is no shortage of parts or servicing expertise for these cars, and all are welcomed at garages which hold a Mercedes-Benz franchise. This is a good thing, because the later models are complex pieces of machinery, and are definitely not the sort of thing for the average DIY enthusiast to attempt to maintain. As even the best-intentioned DIY owner may not have kept a car up to Stuttgart's own high standards, it is always advisable when buying a secondhand vehicle to choose one with a known service history and documents to prove it. The Daimler-Benz network runs its own excellent used-car guarantee scheme, and it is always a good thing to buy a car with this guarantee.

So is there nothing here for the DIY enthusiast? That depends entirely on the skills and patience of the individual. Those in any doubt should avoid the fuel-injected models for a start, and should remember that the more exotic models are very complicated indeed. As a 450SEL 6.9 is not a car to be worked on in the road on a Sunday morning, enthusiasts without better facilities are well-advised to make their choice from among the more mundane models. Eventually, as these cars become older and less commonly seen by Mercedes-Benz dealers, enthusiastic specialists will spring up who will have the necessary expertise to maintain them in good condition. For the present, though, it is best to leave it to the franchised dealers.

With all these dreadful warnings in mind, anyone who wants to purchase a modern Mercedes-Benz may care to re-read the chapters which precede this one, in order to assist in the choice of model. Further assistance is available in Appendix C, where performance figures obtained by the leading motoring journals from road tests will help to evaluate such equations as acceleration versus economy. Is it *really* worth paying extra for a 140mph car when the cheaper version is capable of 120mph and the maximum legal speed limit is 70mph (in Great Britain) or 55mph (in the USA)? Does that extra tenth of a second off the 0-60mph time *really* matter in everyday driving? Only the individual can tell. Once a choice has been made, though, the potential buyer probably wants to know the weaknesses of the chosen model.

Factory-applied rustproofing measures were very thorough on

the Mercedes-Benz cars of the 1970s and early 1980s, and got better as time went on. For this reason, the condition of the bodywork on all models can be a useful guide to the general condition of a car: excessive rust or corrosion in unusual places will suggest that a car has been neglected or has been in an accident and poorly repaired. Authorized Mercedes-Benz dealers *always* rustproof panels repaired or replaced after damage; other garages may not. Lacking the plastic lower panels fitted to many of the latest products from Stuttgart, W107s, W116s and W123s may all rust in the sills and around the wheelarches. W123s, especially the earlier ones, sometimes get rot in the door bottoms if drain holes have become blocked. W107s sometimes suffer in the area of the headlights, W116s on the sharp edges near the front and rear bumper recesses, and W123s around the air intake below the front bumper: in all cases these are areas which very often do not get thoroughly cleaned and so can be prone to the build-up of dirt and mud. Leaking rubber seals in all models can lead to corrosion in the floorpan (door seals) and boot floor (boot-lid seal), so carpets and floor covering should always be lifted to check for this type of problem.

Interior condition tells its own story. In any case, the materials used are generally very hard-wearing. Very important indeed, though, is to check the various items of luxury equipment fitted to a car for correct functioning. Electric window lifts, electrically-powered sunroofs, vacuum seat-back locks on coupe models, and vacuum-operated central locking systems are all astonishingly expensive to repair if they do not work properly. This applies to all models under consideration in this book, and it bears repetition that the more equipment a car has, the more there is to go wrong. Under the heading of 'equipment', incidentally, should also come the alloy wheels, which were standard on some models and optional on others. The pre-1984 design are attractive, but very difficult to keep clean and looking good; the standard hubcaps are much easier to keep clean, but they do present a temptation to thieves, and are expensive to replace.

Mercedes-Benz engines are built to last, and will do so provided they are properly maintained. None of the four, six, or eight-cylinder petrol engines, or the four, five and six-cylinder diesel engines in production since 1970 has any really major weaknesses, and mileages of 120,000 or so before major overhaul are quite commonplace. On the all-alloy engines, however, it is important that the correct corrosion inhibitor has always been used in the cooling system, or damaged waterways may lead to overheating. Yet despite the sophistication and general air of luxury about the bigger-engined Mercedes-Benz models, even the V8s are quite noisy power units. The smaller petrol units are noisier still (it is a characteristic of OHC designs), and the diesels are the worst. Even so, once on the move, all Mercedes-Benz models should be fairly quiet, and even the diesels are usually unrecognizable as such by noise alone above about 30mph. Especially loud noises will indicate problems as in any other engines, and none of the power units, petrol or diesel, should consume very much oil. High-mileage examples will inevitably use more oil than newer and 'tighter' engines, of course.

It has already been said that the do-it-yourself mechanic is advised to steer clear of the fuel-injected engines, which require expert maintenance to keep in tune. Poor fuel consumption figures or starting and idling troubles will warn of maladjusted systems, and it is worth remembering that the extremely sophisticated systems fitted to the later models are not only impossible for the average enthusiast to tune at home, but are also very expensive to rebuild or replace. Complete replacement is fortunately rarely necessary, but it is not unknown.

Transmissions, like engines, are very robust. Manual gearboxes have no special peculiarities, and should operate quietly and smoothly with no feeling of notchiness, although the pre-1976 five-speed boxes can sometimes be a little rough. Automatics should be very smooth in operation, be they three or four-speed units, although the early four-speeders with fluid coupling instead of torque converter can give rather harsher changes. On later boxes, though, rough changes mean trouble – perhaps only adjustment, but quite likely worn friction components or clogged hydraulic valving. Slippage on full-bore starts is a sure sign of a fault. Repairs, as with everything else on these cars, can be very expensive. It is worth remembering that post-Energy Concept automatics give a part-throttle kickdown much more readily than earlier boxes, and that this characteristic is not a fault.

Further back down the drivetrain, rear axles should without exception run quietly. The all-disc, power-assisted braking systems are extremely efficient, but corrosion of the discs can sometimes occur, and a pull to one side may indicate partial seizure of the caliper pistons. Both faults are more likely in a car which has been standing idle or only used infrequently. Pad life can be as low as 5,000 miles on a hard-driven W107, or as high as 20,000 miles on a more sedately conducted saloon. Power-assisted steering systems do not commonly leak, but fluid level checks should in any case be made on a potential purchase. Steering, whether power-assisted or not, is usually both light and positive, although non-power systems can be rather heavy at parking speeds. Vagueness or strange knocking noises may be caused by loose steering-box bolts, which may be found in a car which has been subjected to hard usage.

The handling of all the cars covered in this guide was taut when they were new, and as suspension parts do not deteriorate to a significant extent there should be no excuse for sloppiness in the handling. W107 suspension will nevertheless feel soft and saloon-like to those unfamiliar with the cars, and the low-speed ride of the big W116 saloons may seem harsh to the uninitiated. Things should smooth out at speed, though, so any peculiarities noted then are certainly cause for worry. Worn dampers may cause high-speed shimmy or bounce over poor surfaces, and the rubber bushes which are so essential to the suspension designs should be carefully inspected. If worn, they may contribute both to the transmission of suspension noise into the bodyshell and to uncertain handling. Cars fitted with self-levelling rear suspension should not sag when heavily laden at the rear. As for the complicated hydro-pneumatic suspension system fitted to 450SEL 6.9 models, it should not normally give trouble except, quite rarely, from leaks. Tyres on all models should be good for around 20,000 miles, although the great weight of the W116 saloons can reduce tyre life to 12,000 miles or so if the cars are driven hard.

There is no substitute for viewing potential purchases in the company of a Mercedes-Benz aficionado who is familiar with the model under consideration, and probably the best way of making contact with such people is through the enthusiasts' clubs. Although the emphasis is on the older models, many enthusiasts also run a modern Mercedes-Benz as an everyday car, as in Daimler-Benz history there are none of those discontinuities which cause enthusiasts for older vehicles to reject as rubbish everything built since 1956 (or 1963, or 1971 . . .). Club addresses do change from time to time, and it is wise to double-check before writing by looking in the magazines devoted to the classic car scene, as well as to enclose an SAE.

In Great Britain, the major club is the Mercedes-Benz Club Ltd, which can be contacted through its Membership Secretary at 75 Theydon Grove, Epping, Essex CM14 6PX. This club issues a well-produced bi-monthly magazine called the *Mercedes-Benz Club Gazette,* and has regional sections covering various parts of the country which meet at regular intervals. In the USA, the principal club is The Mercedes-Benz Club of America Inc, which operates from PO Box 9985, Colorado Springs, Colorado 80932. The splendid magazine produced by this club is also bi-monthly and is called *The Star*. Over 70 regional sections cover the USA and Canada, and arrange a wide variety of social events.

Enthusiasts anxious to broaden their knowledge of the modern Mercedes-Benz may wish to know of other books on the subject. The W107s are dealt with in L.J.K. Setright's *Mercedes-Benz Roadsters,* while the eight-cylinder W116 models are covered in F. Wilson McComb's *Mercedes-Benz V8s*; both books are published by Osprey in their *AutoHistory* series. Geoffrey Howard's *Mercedes-Benz S-class,* issued by Cadogan Publications in London, contains some interesting material on its main theme, but also digresses to cover customizing and the 190E 2.3-16. Volume 5 of the excellent German-text BLV Verlagsgesellschaft series by Heribert Hofner deals with the W107s and W116s, and has an interesting chapter on the C-111. Finally, road tests and other articles from the motoring journals are reprinted in two volumes published by Brooklands Books in England. The subject-matter of *Mercedes-Benz 350/450SL and SLC, 1971-1980* and of *Road & Track on Mercedes-Benz, 1970-1980* is self-explanatory, but it should be noted that, contrary to Brooklands Books' usual policy, some articles appear in both volumes.

Broadening the range for the 1980s . . . . .

With the introduction of the W201 series of compact saloons in 1982 Daimler-Benz was able to enter new territory, the cars being specifically aimed at the younger executive. Although the base model 190, with a carburettor-equipped 1.9-litre engine, had far from sparkling performance, no such criticism could be aimed at this exotic derivative of the theme, the 190E 2.3-16, featuring a 16-valve cylinder head developed by Cosworth Engineering. This was one of the first right-hand-drive examples to arrive in the UK in 1985.

The W123 models had been replaced in the mid-1980s by a new W124 series which, unlike the W201 series from which the new range had been evolved, would soon include estate versions. This is the 300TE, powered by the 3-litre single-OHC six-cylinder engine which had replaced the 2.8-litre twin-OHC 'six'.

The W126 S-class saloons had first been seen in a choice of 2.8-litre six-cylinder and 3.8 and 5-litre V8 engine sizes on its introduction towards the end of 1979, but a major revision of the range six years later saw the substitution of the smaller engines by 3-litre 'six' and 4.2-litre V8 power units, accompanied by new wheels and other detail styling changes.

The SEC coupe versions of the S-class cars also received V8 engine transplants, the 380SEC becoming the 420SEC, although the 500SEC remained in the catalogue. As on the saloons, different wheels and changes to the airdams and lower body side panels identified the new models.

APPENDIX A
Technical specifications

Note: All models covered in this Appendix are of unitary (chassisless) construction. Basic data given is for European-specification cars, except where models are US-market only.

280SL, pilot-build May 1974; produced August 1974 – October 1985 (W107)

Engine: Type M110 6-cyl, 86mm bore × 78.8mm stroke, 2,746cc DOHC. Compression ratio 9:1 (8:1 optional; 8.7:1 standard from June 1976; 9:1 from April 1978). 7-bearing crankshaft. Bosch D-Jetronic electronic fuel injection (Bosch K-Jetronic mechanical fuel injection from June 1976). Maximum power 185bhp DIN at 6,000rpm (low-compression engine 170bhp at 6,000rpm; 177bhp at 6,000rpm from June 1976; 185bhp at 5,800rpm from April 1978); maximum torque 170lb/ft at 4,500rpm (166lb/ft at 4,500rpm from June 1976; 171lb/ft at 4,500rpm from April 1978).
Transmission: Single-dry-plate clutch. 4-speed and reverse all-synchromesh gearbox; gear ratios 3.90:1, 2.30:1, 1.41:1, 1.00:1, reverse 3.66:1. Optional 5-speed manual and 4-speed automatic transmissions; gear ratios (5-speed) 3.96:1, 2.34:1, 1.43:1, 1.00:1, 0.88:1, reverse 3.72:1; (automatic) 3.98:1, 2.39:1, 1.46:1, 1.00:1, reverse 5.48:1. 5-speed manual standard from spring 1981; gear ratios 3.82:1, 2.20:1, 1.40:1, 1.00:1, 0.81:1, reverse 3.71:1; gear ratios of automatic (after spring 1981) 3.68:1, 2.41:1, 1.44:1, 1.00:1, reverse 5.14:1. Axle ratio 3.69:1 (early 5-speed models 3.92:1; 3.58:1 on all models from spring 1981). Optional limited-slip differential.
Running gear: Independent front suspension with twin wishbones, coil springs with rubber auxiliary springs and anti-roll bar. Independent rear suspension with semi-trailing arms and coil springs with rubber auxiliary springs and anti-roll bar. Telescopic shock absorbers on all wheels. Power-assisted recirculating-ball steering with 15.6:1 ratio. 4-wheel disc brakes, ventilated at front, with servo assistance and dual hydraulic circuit. ABS braking system optional from 1980. Tyres 185 HR 14 or 195/70 VR 14 (standard from 1980) or 205/70 VR 14.
Dimensions: Wheelbase 96.9in, front track 57.2in, rear track 56.7in, length 172.4in, width 70.5in, height 51.2in, ground clearance 5.5in. Weight 3,307lb. Turning circle 33.9ft.

280SLC, pilot-build May 1974; produced September 1974 – September 1981 (W107)

As 280SL, except:
Dimensions: Wheelbase 111in, length 186.6in. Weight 3,415lb. Turning circle 37.9ft.

300SL, pilot build August 1985; produced from November 1985 (W107)

As 280SL, except:
Engine: Type M103 6-cyl, 88.5mm bore × 82.2mm stroke, 2,962cc OHC. Compression ratio 10:1. 4-bearing crankshaft. Bosch KE-Jetronic fuel injection. Maximum power 190bhp at 5,600rpm; maximum torque 192lb/ft at 4,250rpm.
Transmission: 4-speed automatic only available. Axle ratio 3.46:1.
Running gear: 205/65 VR 15 tyres.
Dimensions: Weight: 3,322lb.

350SL, pilot-build November 1970; produced February 1971 – February 1980 (W107)

As 280SL, except:
Engine: Type M116 V8-cyl, 92mm bore × 65.8mm stroke, 3,499cc OHC. Compression ratio 9.5:1 (7.5:1 optional; 9:1 from January 1976). 5-bearing crankshaft. Bosch D-Jetronic electronic fuel injection (K-Jetronic mechanical fuel injection from January 1976). Maximum power 200bhp DIN at 5,800rpm (180bhp at 5,500rpm for low-compression engine; 195bhp at 5,500rpm from January 1976; 205bhp at 5,750rpm from early 1978); maximum torque 211lb/ft at 4,000rpm (202.5lb/ft at 4,000rpm from January 1976; 209.8lb/ft at 4,000rpm from early 1978).
Transmission: 4-speed all-synchromesh gearbox with reverse; gear ratios 3.96:1, 2.34:1, 1.43:1, 1.00:1, reverse 3.72:1. Optional 4-speed and reverse automatic transmission with fluid coupling; gear ratios 3.98:1, 2.39:1, 1.46:1, 1.00:1, reverse 5.48:1 (3-speed and reverse with torque converter from July 1972; gear ratios 2.31:1, 1.46:1, 1.00:1, reverse 1.84:1). Axle ratio 3.46:1.
Running gear: Tyres 205/70 VR 14.
Dimensions: Weight 3,487lb.

350SLC, pilot-build June 1971; produced February 1972 – March 1980 (W107)

As 350SL, except:
Dimensions: Wheelbase 111in, length 186.6in. Weight 3,597lb. Turning circle 37.9ft.

380SL, pilot-build February 1980; produced May 1980 – October 1985 (W107)

As 350SL, except:
Engine: Type M116 V8-cyl, 92mm bore × 71.8mm stroke, 3,818cc OHC.

Compression ratio 9:1 (7.5:1 optional). 5-bearing crankshaft. Bosch K-Jetronic mechanical fuel injection. Maximum power 218bhp DIN at 5,500rpm (low-compression engine 197bhp at 5,500rpm); maximum torque 224.3lb/ft at 4,000rpm.
From spring 1981, and all US models: Type M116 V8-cyl, 88mm bore × 78.9mm stroke, 3,839cc OHC. Compression ratio 9.4:1 (8.3:1 for USA). 5-bearing crankshaft. Bosch K-Jetronic mechanical fuel injection. Maximum power 204bhp DIN at 5,250rpm (155bhp SAE at 4,750rpm for USA); maximum torque 225lb/ft at 3,250rpm (196lb/ft at 2,750rpm for USA).
Transmission: 4-speed and reverse automatic with torque converter; gear ratios 3.68:1, 2.41:1, 1.44:1, 1.00:1, reverse 5.14:1. Axle ratio 3.27:1 (from spring 1981 and all US models, 2.47:1).
Running gear: ABS braking system optional from 1980. HR tyres (US models).
Dimensions: Length 182.3in (US models). Weight 3,392lb (3,605lb US models).

380SLC, pilot-build February 1980; produced March 1980 – August 1981 (W107)

As 380SL, except:
Dimensions: Wheelbase 111in, length 186.6in (196.4in, US models). Weight 3,435lb (3,585lb, US models). Turning circle 37.9ft.

420SL, pilot-build August 1985; produced from November 1985 (W107)

As 300SL, except:
Engine: Type M116 V8-cyl, 92mm bore × 78.9mm stroke, 4,196cc OHC. Compression ratio 9:1. 5-bearing crankshaft. Bosch CIS-E fuel injection. Maximum power 218bhp DIN at 5,200rpm; maximum torque 236lb/ft at 3,750rpm.
Dimensions: Weight 3,520lb.

350SL 4.5, pilot-build March 1971; produced May 1971 – March 1973; 450SL, produced March 1973 – November 1980 (W107)

As 350SL, except:
Engine: Type M117 V8-cyl, 92mm bore × 85mm stroke, 4,520cc OHC. Compression ratio 8.8:1 (7.5:1 optional; 8:1 for USA). 5-bearing crankshaft. Bosch D-Jetronic electronic fuel injection (Bosch K-Jetronic mechanical fuel injection from November 1975). Maximum power 225bhp DIN at 5,000rpm (low-compression engine 210bhp at 4,800rpm; 180bhp at 4,750rpm for USA; 160bhp SAE at 4,200rpm for USA from 1979; European engine 217bhp DIN at 5,000rpm from November 1975; 225bhp at 5,000rpm from 1978); maximum torque 278lb/ft at 3,000rpm (220lb/ft at 3,000rpm for USA; 230lb/ft at 2,500rpm for USA from 1979; European engine 257lb/ft at 3,250rpm from November 1975; 263lb/ft at 3,250rpm from 1978).
Transmission: 3-speed and reverse automatic with torque converter; gear ratios as for 350SL. Axle ratio 3.07:1 (3.06:1 for USA from 1979; 2.65:1 for USA from 1980).
Dimensions: Weight 3,487lb (3,780lb, US models).

350SLC for USA and 450SLC, pilot-build February 1972; produced July 1972 – October 1980 (W107)

As 350SL 4.5/450SL, except:
Dimensions: Wheelbase 111in, Length 186.6in (196.4in, US models). Weight 3,586lb (3,817lb, US models; 3,860lb, US models 1977; 3,795lb, US models 1979; 3,750lb, US models 1980). Turning circle 37.9ft.

450SLC 5.0, pilot-build September 1977; produced April 1978 – September 1981 (W107)

As 450SLC, except:
Engine: Type M117 V8-cyl, 97mm bore × 85mm stroke, 5,025cc OHC. Compression ratio 8.8:1. 5-bearing crankshaft. Bosch K-Jetronic mechanical fuel injection. Maximum power 240bhp DIN at 5,000rpm; maximum torque 297lb/ft at 3,200rpm.
Transmission: Axle ratio 2.72:1.
Dimensions: Weight 3,333lb.

500SL, produced from April 1980 (W107)

As 450SL, except:
Engine: Type M117 V8-cyl, 96.5mm bore × 85mm stroke, 4,973cc. Compression ratio 8.8:1 (7.5:1 optional; 9.2:1 from spring 1981). 5-bearing crankshaft. Bosch K-Jetronic mechanical fuel injection (Bosch CIS-E fuel injection from autumn 1985). Maximum power 240bhp DIN at 5,000rpm (low-compression engine 225bhp at 4,750rpm; 213bhp at 4,750rpm from spring 1981; 245bhp at 4,750rpm from autumn 1985); maximum torque 298lb/ft at 3,200rpm (288lb/ft at 3,000rpm from November 1981; 286lb/ft at 3,750rpm from autumn 1985).
Transmission: 4-speed and reverse automatic with torque converter; gear ratios as for 380SL. Axle ratio 2.72:1 (2.24:1 from spring 1981).
Dimensions: Weight 3,395lb.

500SLC, pilot-build February 1980; produced March 1980 – July 1981 (W107)

As 500SL, except:
Dimensions: Wheelbase 111in, length 186.6in. Weight 3,454lb. Turning circle 37.9ft.

280S, pilot-build August 1972; produced September 1972 – July 1980 (W116)

Engne: Type M110 6-cyl, 86mm bore × 78.8mm stroke, 2,746cc DOHC. Compression ratio 9:1 (8:1 for USA; 8.7:1 from June 1976). 7-bearing crankshaft. Single Solex 4A1 dual downdraught carburettor. Maximum power 160bhp DIN at 5,500rpm (US models 120bhp at 4,800rpm; Californian models 123bhp at 5,000rpm from 1975; European models 156bhp DIN at 5,500rpm from June 1976); maximum torque 166.4lb/ft at 4,000rpm (112.1lb/ft at 2,800rpm for US models; 143lb/ft at 3,600rpm for Californian models from 1975; 159lb/ft at 4,000rpm for European models from June 1976).

Transmission: Single-dry-plate clutch. 4-speed and reverse all-synchromesh gearbox; gear ratios 3.90:1, 2.30:1, 1.41:1, 1.00:1, reverse 3.66:1. Optional 5-speed and reverse all-synchromesh gearbox; gear ratios 3.96:1, 2.34:1, 1.43:1, 1.00:1, 0.88:1, reverse 3.72:1. Optional 4-speed automatic transmission with torque converter; gear ratios 3.98:1, 2.39:1, 1.46:1, 1.00:1, reverse 5.48:1. Axle ratio 3.69:1 (3.92:1 with 5-speed gearbox).
Running gear: Independent front suspension with unequal length wishbones, coil springs with auxiliary rubber springs, hydraulic telescopic shock absorbers and anti-roll bar. Independent rear suspension with semi-trailing arms, coil springs with auxiliary rubber springs, hydraulic telescopic shock absorbers and anti-roll bar; optional self-levelling strut. Power-assisted recirculating-ball steering with 14:1 ratio. Twin-circuit servo-assisted disc brakes on all wheels, ventilated at front; ABS braking system optional from 1979. 185 HR 14 tyres.
Dimensions: Wheelbase 112.8in, front track 60in, rear track 59.3in, length 195.3in (205.5in, US models), width 73.4in, height 56.1in, ground clearance 5.9in. Weight 3,542lb (manual), 3,630lb (automatic), 3,890lb (US models). Turning circle 37.4ft.

280SE, pilot-build August 1972; produced September 1972 – July 1980 (W116)

As 280S, except:
Engine: Compression ratio 9:1 from April 1978. Bosch D-Jetronic electronic fuel injection (K-Jetronic mechanical fuel injection from early 1976). Maximum power 185bhp DIN at 6,000rpm (177bhp at 6,000rpm from early 1976; 142bhp at 5,750rpm, US Federal models; 137bhp at 5,750rpm, Californian models; 185bhp DIN at 5,800rpm, European models from April 1978; 140bhp at 5,500rpm, US models from 1980); maximum torque 176lb/ft at 4,500rpm; 167lb/ft at 4,500rpm from early 1976; 149lb/ft at 4,600rpm, US Federal models; 142lb/ft at 4,600rpm, Californian models; 171lb/ft at 4,500rpm, European models from April 1978).
Transmission: Axle ratio 3.58:1 (US models from 1978).
Dimensions: Weight 3,542lb (manual), 3,630lb (automatic), 3,905lb (US models, 1977), 3,560lb (US models, 1978), 3,820lb (US models, 1979), 3,795lb (US models, 1980).

280SEL, pilot-build October 1973; produced January 1974 – May 1980 (W116)

As 280SE, except:
Dimensions: Wheelbase 116.7in, length 199.2in. Weight 3,619lb (manual), 3,707lb (automatic). Turning circle 39ft.

300SD, pilot-build February 1977; produced May 1978 – September 1980 (W116)

As 280SE, except:
Engine: Type OM617 5-cyl diesel, 90.9mm bore × 92.4mm stroke, 2,998cc OHC. Compression ratio 21.5:1. 6-bearing crankshaft. Bosch 5-plunger injection pump with Garrett exhaust-driven turbocharger. Maximum power 115bhp DIN at 4,200rpm (120bhp at 4,350rpm for 1980); maximum torque 168lb/ft at 2,400rpm (170lb/ft at 2,400rpm for 1980).
Transmission: 4-speed and reverse automatic transmission with torque converter; gear ratios as for 280SE. Axle ratio 3.07:1.
Running gear: No ABS option.
Dimensions: Length 205.5in. Weight 3,883lb (3,773lb for 1980).

350SE, pilot-build March 1972; produced August 1972 – September 1980 (W116)

As 280S, except
Engine: Type M116 V8-cyl, 92mm bore × 65.8mm stroke, 3,499cc OHC. Compression ratio 9.5:1 (7.5:1 optional; 9:1 from January 1976). 5-bearing crankshaft. Bosch D-Jetronic electronic fuel injection (K-Jetronic mechanical fuel injection from January 1976). Maximum power 200bhp DIN at 5,800rpm (low-compression engine 180bhp at 5,500rpm; 195bhp at 5,500rpm from January 1976; 205bhp at 5,750rpm from January 1978); maximum torque 204lb/ft at 4,000rpm (196lb/ft at 4,000rpm from January 1976; 203lb/ft at 4,000rpm from January 1978).
Transmission: 4-speed and reverse all-synchromesh gearbox; gear ratios 3.96:1, 2.34:1, 1.43:1, 1.00:1, reverse 3.72:1. Optional 3-speed and reverse automatic transmission with torque converter; gear ratios 2.31:1, 1.46:1, 1.00:1, reverse 1.84:1. Axle ratio 3.46:1. Optional limited-slip differential.
Running gear: 205/70 HR 14 tyres.
Dimensions: Weight 3,685lb (manual), 3,773lb (automatic).

350SEL, pilot-build September 1973; produced November 1973 – June 1980 (W116)

As 350SE, except:
Dimensions: Wheelbase 116.7in, length 199.2in. Weight 3,740lb (manual), 3,828lb (automatic). Turning circle 39ft.

450SE, pilot-build August 1972; produced December 1972 – April 1980 (W116)

As 350SE, except:
Engine: Type M117 V8-cyl, 92mm bore × 85mm stroke, 4,520cc OHC. Compression ratio 8.8:1 (7.5:1 optional; 8:1 for USA). 5-bearing crankshaft. Bosch D-Jetronic electronic fuel injection (K-Jetronic mechanical fuel injection from November 1975). Maximum power 225bhp DIN at 5,000rpm (low-compression engine 210bhp at 4,800rpm; 180bhp at 4,750rpm, US Federal models; 170bhp at 4,750rpm, Californian models from 1975; 217bhp at 5,000rpm from November 1975; low-compression engine 200bhp at 4,750rpm from November 1975; 180bhp at 4,800rpm, US models from November 1975; 225bhp at 5,000rpm from January 1978); maximum torque 278.5lb/ft at 3,000rpm (238.8lb/ft at 3,000rpm, US models; 232lb/ft, Californian models from 1975; 265lb/ft at 3,250rpm from November 1975; 220lb/ft, US models from 1977; 257lb/ft at 3,250rpm from January 1978; 230lb/ft at 2,500rpm from 1979).

Transmission: 3-speed automatic only available; gear ratios as for 350SE. Axle ratio 3.07:1.
Dimensions: Weight 3,828lb (manual); 3,946lb (automatic), 4,070lb (US models).

450SEL, produced December 1972 – June 1980 (W116)
As 450SE, except:
Dimensions: Wheelbase 116.7in, length 199.2in (US models 209.4in). Weight 3,828lb (manual), 3,916lb (automatic), 4,100lb (US models), 4,080lb (US models, 1977), 3,975lb (US models, 1980). Turning circle 39ft.

450SEL 6.9, pilot-build February 1975; produced September 1975 – May 1980 (W116)
As 450SEL, except:
Engine: Type M100 V8-cyl, 107mm bore × 95mm stroke, 6,834cc OHC. Compression ratio 8.8:1. 5-bearing crankshaft. Bosch K-Jetronic mechanical fuel injection. Maximum power 286bhp DIN at 4,250rpm (250bhp at 4,000rpm, US models); maximum torque 405lb/ft at 3,000rpm (360lb/ft at 2,500rpm, US models).
Transmission: Axle ratio 2.65:1. Limited-slip differential.
Running gear: Independent front suspension with unequal-length wishbones and self-levelling hydro-pneumatic springs with gas-filled dampers and anti-roll bar. Independent rear suspension with semi-trailing arms, self-levelling hydro-pneumatic springs with gas-filled dampers and anti-roll bar. 215/70 VR 14 tyres.
Dimensions: Weight 4,257lb, 4,390lb (US models), 4,435lb (US models, 1979).

200, pilot-build July 1975; produced February 1976 – November 1985 (W123)
Engine: (1976-1980) Type M115 4-cyl, 87mm bore × 83.6mm stroke, 1,988cc OHC. Compression ratio 9:1 (8:1 optional). 5-bearing crankshaft. Single Stromberg 175CDT carburettor. Maximum power 94bhp DIN at 4,800rpm (low-compression engine 84bhp at 4,800rpm); maximum torque 113lb/ft at 3,000rpm.
(1979-1985) Type M102 4-cyl, 89mm bore × 80.25mm stroke, 1,997cc OHC. Compression ratio 9:1. 5-bearing crankshaft. Single Stromberg 175CDT carburettor. Maximum power 109bhp DIN at 5,200rpm; maximum torque 121lb/ft at 3,000rpm.
Transmission: (1976-1980) Single-dry-plate clutch. 4-speed and reverse all-synchromesh gearbox; gear ratios 3.90:1, 2.30:1, 1.41:1, 1.00:1, reverse 3.66:1. Optional 4-speed and reverse automatic transmission with torque converter; gear ratios 3.98:1, 2.39:1, 1.46:1, 1.00:1, reverse 5.48:1. Axle ratio 3.92:1.
(1979-1985) Single-dry-plate clutch. 4-speed and reverse all-synchromesh gearbox; gear ratios 3.91:1, 2.32:1, 1.42:1, 1.00:1, reverse 3.78:1. Optional 5-speed and reverse all-synchromesh gearbox from February 1982; gear ratios 3.82:1, 2.20:1, 1.40:1, 1.00:1, 0.81:1, reverse 3,71:1. Optional automatic transmission as 1976-1980 models. Axle ratio 3.69:1.
Running gear: Independent front suspension with twin wishbones, coil springs, hydraulic telescopic shock absorbers and anti-roll bar. Independent rear suspension with semi-trailing arms, coil springs, hydraulic telescopic shock absorbers and anti-roll bar; optional hydro-pneumatic self-levelling. Recirculating-ball steering with 22.4:1 ratio; optional power-assisted steering with 14.2:1 ratio (power steering standard from September 1982). 4-wheel disc brakes with servo assistance and dual hydraulic circuit; ABS braking system optional from August 1980. 175 SR 14 tyres.
Dimensions: Wheelbase 110in, front track 58.6in, rear track 56.9in, length 186in, width 70.3in, height 56.6in. Weight 2,954lb. Turning circle 37ft.

200T, pilot-build May 1980; produced November 1980 – November 1985 (W123)
As 200, except:
Running gear: Gas-filled telescopic shock absorbers all round; hydro-pneumatic self-levelling standard. 195/70 SR 14 tyres.
Dimensions: Height 57.9in (over roof rack). Weight 3,241lb, 3,296lb (heavy-duty models).

200D, pilot-build July 1975; produced February 1976 – November 1985 (W123)
As 200, except:
Engine: Type OM615 4-cyl diesel, 87mm bore × 83.6mm stroke, 1,988cc OHC. Compression ratio 21:1. 5-bearing crankshaft. Bosch 4-plunger injection pump. Maximum power 55bhp DIN at 4,200rpm (60bhp at 4,200rpm from February 1979); maximum torque 80lb/ft at 2,400rpm.
Transmission: 4-speed and reverse all-synchromesh gearbox; gear ratios 3.90:1, 2.30:1, 1.41:1, 1.00:1, reverse 3.66:1. Optional 4-speed automatic; optional 5-speed manual from February 1982. Axle ratio (all types) 3.92:1.
Dimensions: Weight 3,146lb (manual), 3,234lb (automatic).

220D, pilot-build July 1975; produced February 1976 – March 1979 (W123)
As 200, except:
Engine: Type OM615 4-cyl diesel, 87mm bore × 92.4mm stroke, 2,197cc OHC. Compression ratio 21:1. 5-bearing crankshaft. Bosch 4-plunger injection pump. Maximum power 64bhp DIN at 4,200rpm; maximum torque 93lb/ft at 2,400rpm.
Transmission: Gear ratios of 4-speed manual box as for 200D.
Dimensions: Weight 3,146lb (manual), 3,234lb (automatic).

230, pilot-build July 1975; produced February 1976 – September 1981 (W123)
As 200, except:
Engine: Type M115 4-cyl, 93.75mm bore × 83.6mm stroke, 2,307cc OHC. Compression ratio 9:1 (8:1 optional). 5-bearing crankshaft. Single

Stromberg 175CDT carburettor. Maximum power 109bhp DIN at 4,800rpm (low-compression engine 95bhp at 4,800rpm); maximum torque 132lb/ft at 3,000rpm.
Transmission: Gear ratios of 4-speed manual box as for 200D. Axle ratio 3.69:1 (3.92:1 on certain special-bodied models with 15-inch wheels).
Dimensions: Length 190.9in (US models). Weight 2,975lb.

230C, pilot-build November 1976; produced June 1977 – June 1980 (W123)

As 230, except:
Running gear: Power-assisted steering standard. 195/70 SR 14 or 195/70 HR 14 tyres.
Dimensions: Wheelbase 106.7in, length 182.7in, height 54.9in. Weight 3,080lb (manual), 3,168lb (automatic). Turning circle 36.1ft.

230T, pilot-build February 1978; produced May 1978 – April 1980 (W123)

As 230, except:
Running gear: Gas-filled shock absorbers all round; hydro-pneumatic self-levelling standard. 195/70 SR 14 tyres (175 HR 15 tyres on heavy-duty model).
Dimensions: Height 57.9in (over roof rack). Weight 3,300lb (manual), 3,388lb (automatic).

230E, pilot-build October 1980; produced July 1972 – November 1985 (W123)

As 200, except:
Engine: Type M102 4-cyl, 95mm bore × 80.25mm stroke, 2,299cc OHC. Compression ratio 9:1. 5-bearing crankshaft. Bosch K-Jetronic mechanical fuel injection. Maximum power 136bhp DIN at 5,100rpm; maximum torque 148lb/ft at 3,500rpm.
Transmission: Axle ratio 3.58:1.
Running gear: Power-assisted steering standard from September 1982. 175 HR 14 tyres.
Dimensions: Weight 2,998lb.

230CE, pilot-build February 1980; produced April 1980 – July 1985 (W123)

As 230E, except:
Running gear: Power-assisted steering standard. 195/70 SR 14 or 195/70 HR 14 tyres.
Dimensions: Wheelbase 106.7in, length 182.7in, height 54.9in. Weight 3,064lb. Turning circle 36.1ft.

230TE, pilot-build October 1979; produced April 1980 – November 1985 (W123)

As 230E, except:
Running gear: Gas-filled shock absorbers all round; hydro-pneumatic self-levelling standard. 195/70 SR 14 or 195/70 HR 14 tyres (175 HR 15 tyres on heavy-duty model).
Dimensions: Height 57.9in (over roof rack). Weight 3,263lb; 3,318lb (heavy-duty models).

240D, pilot-build July 1975; produced February 1976 – November 1985 (W123)

As 200, except:
Engine: Type OM616 4-cyl diesel, 91mm bore × 92.4mm stroke, 2,404cc OHC. Compression ratio 21:1. 5-bearing crankshaft. Bosch 4-plunger injection pump. Maximum power 65bhp DIN at 4,200rpm (74bhp at 4,400rpm from February 1979); maximum torque 98lb/ft at 2,400rpm.
Transmission: Axle ratio 3.69:1.
Running gear: Hydro-pneumatic self-levelling on rear axle standard (long-wheelbase models only); 185 R 15 tyres (long-wheelbase models and certain special-bodied variants).
Dimensions: Wheelbase 134.8in (long-wheelbase models). Weight 3,075lb; 3,450lb (long-wheelbase models). Turning circle 43.5ft (long-wheelbase models).

240TD, pilot-build February 1978; produced May 1978 – November 1985 (W123)

As 240D, except:
Running gear: Gas-filled telescopic shock absorbers all round; hydro-pneumatic self-levelling standard. 195/70 SR 14 tyres (175 HR 15 on heavy-duty models).
Dimensions: Height 57.9in (over roof rack). Weight 3,340lb; 3,395lb (heavy-duty models).

250, pilot-build July 1975; produced April 1976 – November 1985 (W123)

As 200, except:
Engine: Type M123 6-cyl, 86mm bore × 72.45mm stroke, 2,525cc OHC. Compression ratio 8.7:1 (9:1 from September 1979). 4-bearing crankshaft. Single Solex 4A1 dual downdraught carburettor. Maximum power 129bhp DIN at 5,500rpm (140bhp at 5,500rpm from September 1979); maximum torque 137lb/ft at 3,500rpm (140lb/ft at 3,500rpm from September 1979).
Transmission: Axle ratio 3.69:1.
Running gear: Hydro-pneumatic self-levelling on rear axle standard (long-wheelbase models only). Power-assisted steering standard from August 1978. 175 SR 14 or 175 HR 14 tyres (185 R 15 on long-wheelbase and certain special-bodied variants).
Dimensions: Wheelbase 134.8in (long-wheelbase models). Weight 2,998lb; 3,395lb (long-wheelbase models). Turning circle 43.5ft (long-wheelbase models).

250T, pilot-build September 1977; produced May 1978 – November 1985 (W123)

As 250, except:
Running gear: Gas-filled telescopic shock absorbers all round. 195/70 HR

14 tyres (175 HR 15 on heavy-duty models).
Dimensions: Height 57.9in (over roof-rack). Weight 3,322lb (manual), 3,410lb (automatic).

280, pilot-build July 1975; produced December 1975 – July 1981 (W123)

As 200, except:
Engine: Type M110 6-cyl, 86mm bore × 78.8mm stroke, 2,746cc DOHC. Compression ratio 8.7:1 (8:1 optional). 7-bearing crankshaft. Single Solex 4A1 dual downdraught carburettor. Maximum power 156bhp DIN at 5,500rpm (low-compression engine 143bhp at 5,500rpm); maximum torque 159lb/ft at 4,000rpm.
Transmission: No 5-speed option. Axle ratio 3.54:1 (3.58:1 available from November 1977).
Running gear: Power-assisted steering standard. 195/70 HR 14 tyres.
Dimensions: Weight 3,311lb (manual), 3,399lb (automatic).

280C, pilot-build November 1976; produced April 1977 – March 1980 (W123)

As 280, except:
Dimensions: Wheelbase 106.7in, length 182.7in, height 54.9in. Weight 3,311lb (manual), 3,399lb (automatic). Turning circle 36.1ft.

280E, pilot-build July 1975; produced December 1975 – November 1985 (W123)

As 280, except:
Engine: Compression ratio 9:1 from early 1978. Bosch K-Jetronic mechanical fuel injection. Maximum power 177bhp DIN at 6,000rpm (185bhp at 5,800rpm from early 1978); maximum torque 164lb/ft at 4,500rpm (168lb/ft at 4,500rpm from early 1978).
Transmission: 5-speed option from February 1982; gear ratios as 200.
Dimensions: Weight 3,322lb (manual), 3,410lb (automatic).

280CE, pilot-build October 1976; produced April 1977 – July 1985 (W123)

As 280E, except:
Dimensions: Wheelbase 106.7in, length 182.7in, height 54.9in. Turning circle 36.1ft.

280TE, pilot-build September 1977; produced May 1978 – November 1985 (W123)

As 280E, except:
Running gear: Gas-filled telescopic shock absorbers all round. Hydro-pneumatic self-levelling on rear axle standard.
Dimensions: Height 57.9in (over roof rack). Weight 3,465lb (manual), 3,553lb (automatic).

300D, pilot-build July 1975; produced February 1976 – November 1985 (W123)

As 200, except:
Engine: Type OM617 5-cyl diesel, 90.9mm bore × 92.4mm stroke, 3,005cc OHC. Compression ratio 21:1. 6-bearing crankshaft. Bosch 5-plunger injection pump. Maximum power 80bhp DIN at 4,000rpm (88bhp at 4,400rpm from September 1979); maximum torque 127lb/ft at 2,400rpm.
Transmission: Axle ratio 3.46:1.
Running gear: Hydro-pneumatic self-levelling on rear axle standard (long-wheelbase and certain special-bodied models only). Power-assisted steering standard. 185 R 15 tyres (long-wheelbase and certain special-bodied models only).
Dimensions: Wheelbase 134.8in (long-wheelbase models), length 190.9in (US models). Weight 3,197lb; 3,696lb (long-wheelbase models). Turning circle 43.5ft (long-wheelbase models).

300CD, pilot-build May 1977; produced September 1977 – August 1981 (W123)

As 300D, except:
Running gear: 195/70 HR 14 tyres.
Dimensions: Wheelbase 106.7in, length 187.5in, height 58.7in. Weight 3,377lb. Turning circle 36.1ft.

300TD, pilot-build September 1977; produced May 1978 – November 1985 (W123)

As 300D, except:
Running gear: Gas-filled telescopic shock absorbers all round. Hydro-pneumatic self-levelling on rear axle standard. 195/70 SR 14 tyres (175 HR 15 tyres for heavy-duty model).
Dimensions: Height 57.9in (over roof-rack). Weight 3,461lb; 3,516lb (heavy-duty models).

300D Turbodiesel, pilot-build July 1981; produced September 1981 – November 1985 (W123)

As 300D, except:
Engine: Type OM617A. Compression ratio 21.5:1. Garrett exhaust-driven turbocharger. Maximum power 125bhp DIN at 4,350rpm (Federal); 118bhp at 4,350rpm (California); maximum torque 184lb/ft at 2,400rpm (Federal), 177lb/ft at 2,400rpm (California).
Transmission: Automatic only available. Axle ratio 3.07:1.
Running gear: 195/70 HR 14 tyres.
Dimensions: Weight 3,515lb.

300CD Turbodiesel, pilot-build July 1981; produced September 1981 – November 1985 (W123)

As 300CD, except:
Engine: As 300D Turbodiesel.
Transmission: As 300D Turbodiesel.
Dimensions: Weight 3,485lb.

300TD Turbodiesel, pilot-build November 1979; produced October 1980 – November 1985 (W123)

As 300TD, except:
Engine: As 300D Turbodiesel.
Transmission: As 300D Turbodiesel.
Running gear: 195/70 SR 14 or 195/70 HR 14 tyres (175 HR 15 tyres for heavy-duty models).
Dimensions: Length 190.9in (US models). Weight 3,630lb (heavy-duty models); 3,750lb (US models).

APPENDIX B

Vehicle number sequences and production figures

All Mercedes-Benz cars built since the beginning of the 1960 season bear a 14-digit identification number, made up as follows:

First 3 digits: Type (as W number)
Second 3 digits: Body type
Next digit: 1 (LHD) or 2 (RHD)
Next digit: 0 (manual transmission), or 2 (automatic)
Last 6 digits: serial number

This vehicle identification number will be found on a plate at the front of the car under the bonnet. A typical vehicle identification number would be 123.053 – 22 – 006160, which by comparison with the full list of sequences given below and the digit code above is seen to be a RHD 280CE coupe with automatic transmission. Note that the year of manufacture is not revealed by the vehicle number.

Type and body type numbers

W107

280SL	280SLC	300SL	350SL	350SLC	380SL	380SLC	420SL
107.042	107.022	107.041	107.043	107.023	107.045	107.025	107.047
350SL 4.5/ 450SL	450SLC	450SLC 5.0	500SL	500SLC			
107.044	107.024	107.026	107.046	107.026			

W116

280S	280SE	280SEL	300SD	350SE	350SEL	450SE	450SEL
116.020	116.024	116.025	116.120	116.028	116.029	116.032	116.033
450SEL 6.9							
116.036							

W123

	200	200 (M102)	200T	200D	220D	230	230E	230C	230CE	230T	230TE
Standard	123.020	123.220	123.280	123.120		123.023	123.223	123.043	123.243	123.083	123.283
Special						123.000					
LWB											

	240D	240TD	250	250T	280	280E	280C	280CE	280TE
Standard	123.123	123.183	123.026			123.033	123.050	123.053	123.093
Special									
LWB	123.125		123.028						

	300D	300CD	300TD	300D Turbodiesel	300CD Turbodiesel	300TD Turbodiesel
Standard	123.130	123.150	123.190	123.133	123.153	123.193
Special						
LWB	123.132					

Production totals
Note: Figures are for calendar-year, not model-year.

W107 models

	350SL	350SLC	350SL 4.5/ 450SL	350SLC (US)/ 450SLC	280SL	280SLC	450SLC 5.0/ 500SLC	380SL	380SLC	500SL	Annual total
1970	3										3
1971	4,802	6	2,131								6,939
1972	4,778	5,562	7,473	700							18,513
1973	1,647	3,750	8,654	5,594							19,645
1974	574	864	6,093	2,961	297	300					11,089
1975	390	589	6,011	2,993	1,020	1,312					12,315
1976	540	671	6,625	3,802	1,099	1,508					14,245
1977	650	822	8,110	4,569	1,347	1,624	9				17,131
1978	743	807	7,434	4,382	1,536	1,553	524				16,979
1979	934	775	8,184	4,510	2,155	1,741	937				19,236
1980	243	79	5,583	2,228	2,429	1,510	816	3,347	1,737	501	18,473
1981					2,628	1,118	483	9,470	2,052	899	16,650
1982					3,165			9,926		1,297	14,388

W116 models

	280S	280SE	350SE	450SE	450SEL	280SEL	350SEL	450SEL 6.9	300SD	Annual total
1972	3,787	3,735	4,353	52	24					11,951
1973	15,340	18,266	14,340	13,400	6,930	1	58			68,335
1974	20,808	18,634	7,226	7,579	8,350	535	529			63,661
1975	21,996	17,376	5,447	4,672	6,167	716	552	474		57,400
1976	18,031	17,968	4,734	5,188	9,650	1,042	718	1,475		58,806
1977	17,080	26,903	5,723	4,223	10,042	1,295	807	1,798	51	67,922
1978	15,307	23,571	4,964	3,570	8,508	1,622	911	1,665	5,970	66,088
1979	9,208	22,568	4,099	2,746	8,217	1,551	653	1,839	13,194	64,075
1980	1,291	1,572	214	174	1,690	270	38	129	9,419	14,797
Total	122,848	150,593	51,100	41,604	59,578	7,032	4,266	7,380	28,634	473,035

W123 models
a) 4-cylinder petrol models

	200 (1,988cc)	200 (1,997cc)	200T	230	230C	230T	230E	230CE	230TE	Annual total
1975	5			9						14
1976	26,374			32,060	1					58,435
1977	39,112			49,426	3,484					92,022
1978	35,884			42,270	7,049	1,793				86,996
1979	34,190	37		47,739	6,538	3,829	31		2	92,366
1980	23,207	17,606	648	23,549	1,603	1,262	24,997	4,818	3,750	101,440

W123 models

a) 4-cylinder petrol models

	200 (1,988cc)	200 (1,997cc)	200T	230	230C	230T	230E	230CE	230TE	Annual total
1981		54,780	3,142	1,132			62,125	7,192	5,655	134,026
1982		60,670	3,809				60,777	6,734	7,158	139,148

b) Diesel models

	200D	220D	240D	240TD	300D	300D Turbo-diesel	300CD	300CD Turbo-diesel	300TD	300TD Turbo-diesel	Annual total
1975	5	4	7		9						25
1976	36,894	16,733	21,247		28,996						103,870
1977	56,378	19,323	40,382		48,605		1,078		1		165,767
1978	49,359	19,230	42,816	3,003	49,908		2,485		3,144		169,945
1979	52,834	1,446	62,678	6,387	52,296		1,834		11,180	2	188,657
1980	56,435		69,908	5,820	50,197		1,770		7,523	1,852	193,505
1981	51,152		73,162	5,078	38,858	4,505	335	777	3,308	6,710	183,885
1982	44,633		74,627	5,881	30,720	20,178		1,985	3,712	6,302	188,038

c) 6-cylinder petrol models

	250	250T	280	280E	280TE	280C	280CE	Annual total
1975	5		957	607				1,569
1976	14,915		12,821	17,638		2	2	45,378
1977	25,183	1	7,530	17,651	3	1,577	6,413	58,358
1978	23,306	1,381	4,103	14,904	1,260	1,243	6,958	53,155
1979	21,798	2,946	3,139	18,363	4,059	757	5,091	56,153
1980	17,447	2,761	3,477	17,703	3,614	125	4,013	49,140
1981	8,029	402	1,179	12,723	1,956		2,774	27,063
1982	5,392	213		10,757	2,545		2,509	21,416

APPENDIX C

How fast? How economical? How heavy?

W107

	350SL (European, 4-sp Auto)	350SL 4.5 (US, 3-sp Auto)	380SLC (European, 4-sp Auto)	450SLC (European, 3-sp Auto)	500SL (European, 4-sp Auto)
Mean maximum speed (mph)	126	124	133	136	140(†)
Acceleration (sec)					
0-30mph	3.7	4.6	3.2	3.5	2.6
0-40mph	5.0	6.2	4.6	5.3	4.0
0-50mph	7.0	8.2	6.3	6.9	5.4
0-60mph	9.3	10.5	8.4	9.0	7.1
0-70mph	12.0	13.8	11.2	11.5	9.1
0-80mph	15.4	17.5	14.1	14.6	11.5
0-90mph	20.0	–	17.6	18.2	14.5
0-100mph	26.0	29.5	23.0	23.2	18.1
Standing ¼-mile (sec)	17.0	17.9	16.5	16.9	15.2
Acceleration on the move (sec)(*)					
10-30mph	3.6 (2)	–	–	3.1 (1)	–
20-40mph	3.5 (2)	–	2.6 (K)	3.7 (1)	2.3 (K)
30-50mph	8.3	–	3.1 (K)	3.6 (1)	2.8 (K)
40-60mph	9.1	–	3.8 (K)	4.0 (1)	3.1 (K)
50-70mph	9.7	–	4.9 (K)	5.0 (2)	3.7 (K)
60-80mph	10.3	–	5.7 (K)	5.6 (2)	4.4 (K)
70-90mph	11.2	–	6.4 (K)	6.8 (2)	5.4 (K)
80-100mph	12.2	–	8.9 (K)	9.6 (2)	6.6 (K)
Overall fuel consumption (mpg)	14.7	–	16.7	14.1	16.1
Typical fuel consumption (mpg)	16,2	13,2	20.0	15.5	–
Unladen weight (lb)	3,405	3,670	3,432	3,685	3,386
Original test published	*Autocar* August 12 1971	*Road & Track* October 1971	*Motor* January 24 1981	*Autocar* October 11 1975	*Motor* April 11 1981

(†) Manufacturer's figure

(*) The high overall gearing and quick-acting kickdowns in the automatic transmissions of many modern Mercedes-Benz make it impossible in some cases to obtain on-the-move acceleration figures in direct top gear. The figures given here represent those for the highest quoted gear in each speed increment. The figure given in parentheses indicates when the time does not represent a direct top gear figure, e.g. (2) = 2nd gear, (K) = kickdown where gear is not specified.

W116

	280SE (European, 4-sp Auto)	300SD (US, 4-sp Auto)	450SEL (European, 3-sp Auto)	450SEL (US, 3-sp Auto)	450SEL 6.9 (European, 3-sp Auto)
Mean maximum speed (mph)	120	110	134	129	140
Acceleration (sec)					
0-30mph	3.6	3.8	3.7	3.7	3.0
0-40mph	5.3	–	5.2	–	4.2
0-50mph	7.3	8.8	7.0	–	5.6
0-60mph	9.7	12.7	9.1	9.3	7.3
0-70mph	13.2	17.6	11.6	–	9.5
0-80mph	16.9	24.5	15.0	14.7	12.0
0-90mph	21.9	–	19.1	–	15.4
0-100mph	29.8	–	24.4	–	19.5
Standing ¼-mile (sec)	17.3	19.3	16.7	17.2	15.4
Acceleration on the move (sec)					
10-30mph	–	–	2.8 (1)	–	2.2 (1)
20-40mph	5.6 (3)	–	4.6 (2)	–	2.2 (1)
30-50mph	6.0 (3)	–	4.7 (2)	–	2.7 (1)
40-60mph	6.4 (3)	–	4.5 (2)	–	3.4 (1)
50-70mph	10.8	–	7.3	–	4.5 (2)
60-80mph	11.9	–	8.0	–	4.7 (2)
70-90mph	13.2	–	8.5	–	6.1 (2)
80-100mph	14.7	–	9.9	–	7.1
Overall fuel consumption (mpg)	16.7	25.0	14.7	15.5-17.0	13.6
Typical fuel consumption (mpg)	18	–	16	–	15
Unladen weight (lb)	3,676	3,885	3.904	3,970	4,060
Original test published	*Autocar* July 12 1973	*Road & Track* August 1978	*Autocar* May 4 1974	*Road & Track* May 1978	*Autocar* March 24 1979

W123

	200 (4-speed manual)	230TE (European, 3-sp Auto)	280E (European, 3-sp Auto)	300D (European, 4-sp Auto)	300CD (US, 4-sp Auto)
Mean maximum speed (mph)	96	106	117	88.4	95
Acceleration (sec)					
0-30mph	4.4	4.3	3.8	4.9	4.7
0-40mph	7.0	6.3	5.6	7.8	–
0-50mph	10.5	9.0	7.7	12.4	11.8
0-60mph	15.3	12.9	10.4	18.5	17.1
0-70mph	21.4	17.2	13.9	27.8	24.8
0-80mph	32.4	23.5	17.9	44.5	37.8
0-90mph	50.1	32.0	23.2	–	–
0-100mph	–	48.3	32.9	–	–
Standing ¼-mile (sec)	20.2	18.6	17.6	21.0	21.2
Acceleration on the move (sec)					
10-30mph	–	3.9 (2)	–	–	–
20-40mph	11.7	6.4 (3)	3.5 (K)	5.4 (K)	–
30-50mph	11.6	9.9	5.1 (K)	7.8 (K)	–
40-60mph	12.0	11.1	6.6 (K)	10.9 (K)	–
50-70mph	13.5	11.7	6.7 (K)	16.0 (K)	–
60-80mph	17.0	13.0	11.3 (K)	27.8 (K)	–
70-90mph	28.3	15.3	–	–	–
80-100mph	–	24.6	17.2 (K)	–	–
Overall fuel consumption (mpg)	22.1	22.5	–	–	24
Typical fuel consumption (mpg)	–	–	21.0	24.2	–
Unladen weight (lb)	2,967	3,444	3,212	3,208	3,520
Original test published	*Autocar* September 16 1978	*Autocar* September 26 1981	*Motor* October 9 1976	*Motor* August 18 1979	*Road & Track* January 1978